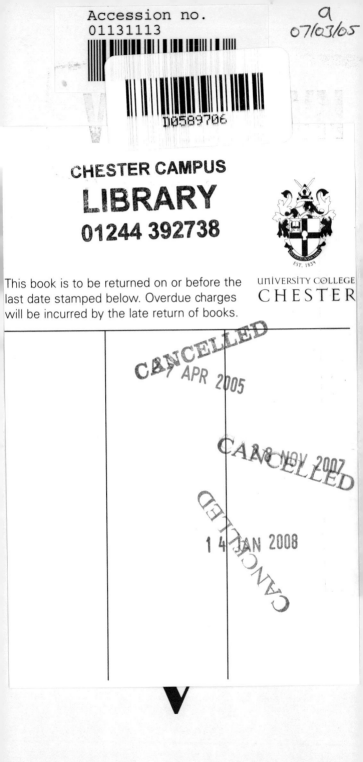

Appearing on the first anniversary of the attacks on the World Trade Center and the Pentagon, these three books from Verso present analyses of the United States, the media, and the events surrounding September 11 by Europe's most stimulating and provocative philosophers. Probing beneath the level of TV commentary, political and cultural orthodoxies, and 'rent-a-quote' punditry, Jean Baudrillard, Paul Virilio and Slavoj Žižek offer three highly original and readable accounts that serve as both fascinating introductions to the direction of their respective projects and insightful critiques of the unfolding events. This series seeks to comprehend the philosophical meaning of September 11 and will leave untouched none of the prevailing views currently propagated.

THE SPIRIT OF TERRORISM
Jean Baudrillard

GROUND ZERO
Paul Virilio

WELCOME TO THE DESERT
OF THE REAL!
Slavoj Žižek

GROUND ZERO

◆

PAUL VIRILIO

Translated by Chris Turner

VERSO

London • New York

This edition first published by Verso 2002
© Verso 2002
Translation © Chris Turner 2002
First published as *Ce qui arrive*
© Éditions Galilée 2002

1 3 5 7 9 10 8 6 4 2

Verso
UK: 6 Meard Street, London W1F 0EG
USA: 180 Varick Street, New York, NY 10014–4606
www.versobooks.com

Verso is the imprint of New Left Books

ISBN 1–85984–416–2

British Library Cataloguing in Publication Data
A catalogue record for this book is available from the British Library

Library of Congress Cataloging-in-Publication Data
A catalog record for this book is available from the Library of Congress

Typeset in Perpetua by M Rules
Printed and bound in the UK by
Biddles Ltd, Guildford and King's Lynn
www.biddles.co.uk

Better to expect the foreseeable
than to be surprised by the unexpected.

André Isaac (Pierre Dac)

1

Science is the only religion of the future.

FRANÇOIS RASPAIL

'"This here Progress," said Mr. Tom Smallways, "it keeps on." "You'd hardly think it could keep on," said Mr. Tom Smallways."[1] And a hundred years after H.G. Wells's hero, one does, indeed, wonder how it still can.

When you look at one of those sets of pictures which, in 1900, claimed to show daily life as it would be in the year 2000, you notice, in fact, that everything which constitutes our current technical environment was there, already planned out – television, computers, the high-speed monorail, the moon rocket, weapons of mass destruction, robotics, home automation, rollerblades in city streets. . . .

Progress, adjusted to the profit motive, seemed finally to have come down to the irruption of a host of machine-toys for

1 H.G. Wells, *The War in the Air*, in *The History of Mr. Polly and The War in the Air*, (London: Odhams Press, undated), p.169.

adults who could, with their aid, do *what they had been forbidden to do as children* – by their size, their lack of muscle, and their intellectual or sexual limitations, but also by parental authority, the rules and taboos of social life, of their culture or religion.

Almost everything technical change was to force on us would be done in the name of this **prohibition to prohibit** which, for each human being, brought on to the stage the child they had once been.

The enthusiasts for Progress, a dangerous gang of dwarves smitten with gigantism, would then come to entertain a scientifically naive conception of the world in which positivism would become a veiled nihilism, and growth a negative growth – the satisfaction of a stubbornly repeated infantile refusal.[2]

After the murder of the *Creator* (the death of God foretold in the nineteenth century) and that of the *procreator* in the following century, it was inevitable that this system of retrogression would end in the demand for a spermless genesis and in the embryonic pre-infantile stage. . . .

And, without even noticing it, the inhabitants of the developed countries would pass, with the end of the Cold War, from the nuclear state to the promise of a state eugenics, from the atomic bomb to the genetic bomb – something which would have been impossible without the 'information bomb'.[3]

---

2 'As early as the first half of the twentieth century, Witold Gombrowicz and a number of his contemporaries had noted that the mark of modernity was not growth or human progress, but rather the refusal to grow up. "Immaturity and infantilism are the most effective categories for defining modern man".' (Paul Virilio, *The Information Bomb*, London: Verso, 2000, p. 94.)

3 That is to say, the impact of information technology. The phrase 'information bomb' was apparently coined by Einstein [Trans.].

'When we have worn out the interest we once took in death, when we realize we have nothing more to gain from it, we fall back on birth, we turn to a much more inexhaustible abyss', wrote E.M. Cioran, author of *The Trouble with Being Born*.[4]

It is in this context that we can see the full meaning of the Perruche ruling by the French Appeal Court on 17 November 2000. For the first time, that higher court granted a disabled adolescent damages intended not as reparation for the serious afflictions from which he suffered – this had already been done on a previous occasion – but for *the harm of being born*.

Shortly after this penalization of birth, the same court had to issue a ruling of principle on the status of the foetus, and we learned on 29 June 2001 that *'the unborn child is not a person and could not, therefore, be regarded as a victim'*.[5]

Which, to put it plainly, means that until a child comes into the world, it cannot be said to be a child and cannot, therefore, be protected by any of our laws.

The decree of 29 June thus backed up the draft law on bioethics announced six months earlier by the French government, and also the founding of an Agency for Procreation, Embryology and Human Genetics – a set of measures which would make it possible, in short order, to turn the human embryo into a *processed good* to be offered for sale.

4 E.M. Cioran, *The Trouble with Being Born*, trans. Richard Howard (New York: Arcade Publishing, 1998), p. 11.
5 'There is no such thing as a baby' was a slogan of the British psychoanalyst D.W. Winnicott, whose radio broadcasts were an immense popular success in the 1950s.

As the biologist Jacques Testart was to point out, following the British initiative to conceive embryos for research purposes: 'France will soon be contributing to a major anthropological step: for the first time in their history, *men are to produce human beings in order to destroy them*.'

Noëlle Lenoir, a constitutional judge for nine years (March 1992–2001), who has, we are told, drafted 'a sound report on bio-ethics', is not reluctant to reveal to the press that 'the Constitutional Council has, in recent times, changed a great deal and has become a genuine Constitutional Court concerning itself with all social questions and this should, shortly, incorporate the international dimension'.[6]

But let us attend, further, to the remarks of the editors of the papers of the Conference on Genetic Heritage and the Rights of Humanity organized in February 1990 with the participation of the European Communities under the distinguished patronage of François Mitterrand.[7] By way of introduction, they said, among other things: 'The researchers in the life and human sciences are, with doctors, jurists, philosophers and decision-makers . . . engaged, in Europe, in making explicit the autonomy of their ethical thought.'

---

6 Interview with Bernard Le Solleu, *Ouest-France*, 12 April 2001. In June, Madame Lenoir was appointed chair of the European Group on Ethics in Sciences and New Technologies of the European Union, which was to rule on the regulation of the use of human cell-tissue.

7 The papers of this conference, held under the auspices of the Commission of the European Communities and the Association Descartes, were edited by Frédéric Gros and Gérard Huber and published as *Vers un anti-destin? Patrimoine génétique et droits de l'humanité* (Paris: Odile Jacob, 1992).

Such a profession of faith is innovative, since ethical and bio-ethical thought have never until now, strictly speaking, been *autonomous*, as every culture, society or religion of any lasting duration has had its own, and every politics has been, a priori, biological. . . .

On the other hand, let us imagine for a moment – as Schopenhauer once invited us to do – the act of generation being neither a need nor a pleasure, but a matter of pure thought and reason. As he goes on to ask, '*Could the human race continue to exist?*'

The numerous conferences and gatherings of all kinds we have seen over the last few years would simply seem to indicate that we shall soon reach this point.[8]

After millennia, not so much of humanism as of (Graeco-Latin and Judaeo-Christian) anthropocentrism, a great schism is in preparation, and we are living through the beginnings of it.

*

When, in the *Handbook of the Hitler Youth*, one reads: 'We are shaping the life of our peoples and our legislation in accordance with the verdicts of genetics', one is tempted to see this old directive of the 'Final Solution' as relating to the most topical of current events, and to resituate it particularly within the context of the 'countdown' of an infantile solipsism, a sectarian fundamentalism turned towards the intimacy of foetal life, *the inexhaustible abyss of every beginning*.

8 See the text of Axel Kahn's statement of Monday 3 September 2001 in Durban during the forum on racism organized by UNESCO.

What some today term the 'new individualism' might merely be the emergence of 'an egotism so colossal that the Universe cannot contain it', as Schopenhauer wrote, after his instructive meeting with Bonaparte in Paris, in the very year the *petit caporal* proclaimed himself emperor. . . .

'Sovereignty of the **ego**' placed at everyone's disposal, by the constantly renewed efforts of domestic technologies – a *folie des grandeurs* quite comparable to that which the alienists of Bâle were to detect in Nietzsche.

Supermen, exceptional men, geniuses, giants, demi-gods, 'men too strong for their social milieu', wrote Nietzsche to Strindberg, that other forgotten precursor of German expressionism.[9] An emotional appeal one could also find at the time in the sensational press, or in serialized popular fiction.

This caricatural cult of abnormality does, however, lose much of its mythic aura if, like the British historian Anthony Blunt, one strives to see it first and foremost as a *social demand*.[10] The demand, in particular, of the Italian artists of the Quattrocento, wishing to extract themselves from the constraints of craft organization and the inferior condition of *manual worker*, from their confraternities and guild traditions –

---

9 Erich F. Podach, *Nietzsches Zusammenbruch. Beiträge zu einer Biographie auf Grund unveröffentlichter Dokumente*, Heidelberg 1930. In this work, Dr Podach opportunely recalls Nietzsche's admiration for Francis Galton. According to Podach, as the son of a pastor and having initially received theological training, he also owed a great debt to the German sectarians of the Reformation period, to the incantatory violence of the Anabaptist Thomas Münzer, Sebastian Frank or Hans Denk . . . those flagellants whom some Germans would soon be comparing with Hitler.

10 See Anthony Blunt, *Artistic Theory in Italy 1450–1600* (Oxford: Clarendon Press, 1956), pp. 48–57 ("The Social Position of the Artist").

and to do so thanks to the host of roles they had ambitions to occupy in the liturgy of the Mediterranean city-states: painters and sculptors, archaeologists and restorers, but also architects, poets, diplomats, anatomists, siege-engineers, engineers, designers of optical apparatus and androids, and so forth.

When Alberti – as a distant disciple of Vitruvius – announces that he aspires to *the totality of knowledge through the mathematical construction of the world*, one can already hear how this new totalitarian will to power on the part of a single man implies the replacement or, beyond that, the destruction of the world as up to that point perceived, re-presented and lived in common by the majority of humankind – that is to say, the mass of manual workers.[11]

These are the underestimated beginnings of an *egocentric revolution,* illustrating far in advance of its time the moving remark which Kafka, in his latter years, was to make to his friend Gustav Janouch: 'Intellectual labour tears a man out of human society. A craft, on the other hand, leads him towards men. What a pity I can no longer work in the workshop or in the garden.'[12]

By contrast, when Leonardo utters his famous phrase '*pittura e cosa mentale*', he is, in the end, expressing his disdain for his painted (manual) work, and he goes on to say: 'It is the superiority of judgement over the possibilities of its application that is the mark of the authentic artist.'

---

11 'the times when 94% of all the mechanical energy produced and consumed on earth was obtained by the muscular force of men and animals', Paul Virilio, *Défense populaire et luttes écologiques* (Paris: Galilée, 1978), pp. 26–27.
12 Gustav Janouch, *Conversations with Kafka*, trans. Goronwy Rees. Second revised and enlarged edition (London: André Deutsch, 1971), p. 15.

Here one finds oneself confronted with a singular way of resolving the old debate on human consciousness – by artists paradoxically casting into doubt the *efficacy of their senses*. In Leonardo one can already hear a Descartes, though one hears, above all, contemporaries of his, such as Jakob Böhme advocating 'life beyond the senses', the mystical ego of inner change and the techno-scientific ego of the changing of the Universe merging here in a single desire to annihilate sensory life, the heterogeneity of our consciousness of the world as such.

*

In a short essay which appeared in 1964, entitled *God & Golem, Inc.*, Norbert Wiener, one of the fathers of cybernetics, reflected on the foundations of computing and artificial intelligence, and invited us to reflect on 'certain points where cybernetics impinges on religion'.[13]

It is very clear that the hypotheses he was venting there are uncomfortable ones for rationalist thought – for the spirit of the Enlightenment, as the phrase goes – since they are hypotheses which are most often automatically omitted from the epistemological debate, when in reality they underpin it.

For example the extremely simple hypothesis of a scientific imagination governed overall by the points where it impinges on Judaeo-Christianity and on a Catholic Church asserting, like Sylvester II, Pope in the year 1000, that 'the Divinity made a considerable present to men by giving them faith and *by not denying them science*'.

---

13 The subtitle to Norbert Wiener's *God & Golem, Inc.* (Cambridge, MA: the MIT Press, 1964).

The sensible and the supra-sensible are not mutually exclusive, but they do not merge either. As Einstein was to write, 'there is no scientific truth', because truth and science are not of the same nature.

After the great Western Schism and the denunciation of the Donation of Constantine (1440), which was to undermine the legal foundations of the temporal and spiritual power of the Roman papacy, we saw in Europe a slow erosion of Mediterranean predominance and a race towards the West, giving rise, particularly in the Germanic countries, to a resurgence of sects rebelling against the Catholic Church, which henceforth took refuge, with its aristocratic luxury and its gold, behind a pomp which aptly reflected the practice of simony, and which, according to Saint Thomas More, had become the enemy of knowledge and a propagator of ignorance.

It is interesting, then, to observe that at the time when the religious Reformation was teaching the return of Christianity to the purity of its biblical origins, and recommending the direct dialogue between each believer and the God of Genesis, the scientific imagination, for its part, was making a quite similar move, a kind of *heretical escape*, engineering the confrontation between the exceptional individual and monotheism – itself constantly coming up against the biblical scenario of the Creation of the Universe in its most orthodox version – and rapidly coming to believe itself alone capable of honouring to the letter the **sicut deus** of the Luciferian bargain, and paying the due price.[14]

14 The reference here is to a lecture given by the young pastor
      Dietrich Bonhoeffer at Berlin university in the winter of 1932–33:

Paradoxically, these antipodal twins, the religious Reformation and the revolution of emergent scientific thought, will advance together. And with the rise of physics and mathematics in the sixteenth century, science will no longer merely write, but enact *a second history of life and death which, without the first, would have no meaning*. The history of *man without limits*, of the human being rid of God, such as pastor Dietrich Bonhoeffer was to denounce in his radio broadcast of 1 February 1933, thus standing out openly against Hitler's claim to total sovereignty only two days after his accession to power. A power of totalitarian extermination which, as Hannah Arendt noted, claimed to be based on a scientific process. . . .

But long before 'the *coup de force* aimed at setting Reason in the place of the Creator God', we saw the iconoclastic wave that swept through Europe from the sixteenth century onwards. For the German or Swiss reformers it was not so much a question of obeying a biblical commandment (which each individual could in conscience observe[15]) as of systematically destroying any visible manifestation of the incarnation of Christ – painted works representing the main episodes of the

'Sicut deus' [Like God]. Bonhoeffer takes as his text 'And the serpent said to the woman: You will not die at all. Instead God knows that on the day you eat from it your eyes will be opened, and you will be like God and know what good and evil is.' (Genesis 3: 1–3). Dietrich Bonhoeffer, *Creation and Fall: A Theological Exposition of Genesis 1–3* (Minneapolis, MN: Fortress Press, 1997), pp. 111–114.

15 *Iconoclasme: vie et mort de l'image médiévale*, an exhibition held at the Musée de l'Oeuvre Notre-Dame, Strasbourg, July–August 2001. See also the reference to the Old Testament commandment here: 'Thou shalt not make unto thee any graven image, or any likeness of any thing that is in heaven above, or that is in the earth beneath, or that is in the water under the earth' (Exodus 20: 4). See also the Cabbalistic tradition.

earthly life of the Man-God of Emmaus, stained-glass windows, sculptures, cult objects: a fundamental cultural break of which Schlegel spoke in his day.

The origin being the final destination of the various Reform movements, behind the pyres of the iconoclastic holocaust – those, for example, of a utopian Calvinism which almost cost Hans Holbein his life – the age-old proposition of human predestination was rediscovered, the prenatal sifting of the pure and the impure, of those well-born and ill-born, according, allegedly, to God's will.

Later, we shall see the same distrust of the act of generation among the English Puritan fanatics (the future pilgrim fathers of the *Mayflower*), and the iconoclastic Cromwell conflating the destruction of sacred works and buildings with the prohibition of the festival of Christmas, the celebration of Christ's coming into the world and freeing the human race from the fatality of death. With still to come, some three hundred years later, the remarks of a Cioran, rounding off his thinking on 'the trouble with being born' with a reminder of the sectarian arguments of the early Christian era, particularly the beliefs of the Danubian peoples, who decreed that, in the Inferno of an Earth that had become Satan's own, to be born and be alive would be calamities, and there would be only one perfect life: the life that escaped any beginning, the life before life which some of them called *prebirth*.[16]

With Christ now occupying only a subaltern place in these new temples, believers would be returned to the ancient

16 During an interview published in February 1999 in *Le Magazine littéraire*, Cioran talks to H.J. Heinrichs about his Romanian origins, and his interest in the Bulgarian Bogomil sects and their diabolization of biogenesis.

despair at being born human, and the act of generation would escape the *principle of indeterminacy* – the doctrine of free will and redemption – defended, with a ferocity we know so well, by the Roman papacy.

It will come as no great surprise, then, to rediscover the same Manichaean beliefs among the nineteenth-century scientists promoting eugenics, evolution, hereditary theories, phrenology and statistical methods . . . those convictions which will become the main ideological tools of the totalitarian systems of the twentieth century.

If, according to François Raspail and many others, 'Science is the only religion of the future', we have to admit that this *scientific integrism* carries in its train a heavy sectarian burden, littered with Gnosticist vestiges organized around a recurrent hatred of matter: what was called the *mortification of the flesh* – that of the human body and, more generally, of the body of the living world.

From the *perspectiva*, the 'seeing-through', of the Quattrocento to the *Utopia* of Saint Thomas More, with its capital named Aircastle, its river Nowater and its cities populated by Nopeople,[17] and with the Cartesian *tabula rasa* or 'progress's dash towards ever greater abstraction' announced by the ethnologist Leroi-Gourhan still to come, the techno-scientific imagination has structured itself for some six hundred years around the **concept of disappearance** – of

17 Here I have followed the translation by Paul Turner: Thomas More, *Utopia* (Harmondsworth: Penguin, 1965). Utopia ('no place') contains a river Anydros ('without water') and a ruler called Ademus ('one who has no people'). In the original French edition of this work, the reference is to the translation by D.A. Grisoni, and to that same author's series of articles on *Utopia* published in *La Vie* in July 2001 [Trans.].

the inexorable enactment of a stripping down of the World, of the substance of the living world.

Techno-scientific solipsism can be seen, then, never to have been anything but a *vehicle for hatred*, elevated into the destiny of a biosphere whose crime would be to have presented itself to us as such.[18]

Just as torture heralds the imminent putting-to-death of the condemned man, so the iconoclasm of the sixteenth century inaugurated a series of historical exterminations – of cultures, laws, peoples, distances, and human time itself. . . .

As for the evolutionist illusion of a Darwinian Progress, it was part of the ideological violence of a system in which *it would not simply be might which prevailed, but the* madness *of the mightiest*.[19]

After a Trotsky declaring in 1933 that 'all the distinctive traits of the races fade before the internal combustion engine, not to speak of the machine-gun', sixty years later there would quite logically be ideologues of Progress like Hans Moravec to assert that, thanks to the newly acquired capabilities of robotics and nano-technologies, 'biological humans would be squeezed out of existence',[20] since 'biological species almost never survive encounters with superior competitors'.[21]

---

18 UNESCO now has listed 'International Biosphere Reserves'; the Parc régional d'Armorique is among them.

19 The French expression used here – 'la Raison deviendrait la folie du plus fort' (a play on the notion of 'la raison du plus fort') – was coined by Ionesco. The dramatist – who, like Cioran, was of Romanian origin – also claimed that 'the world cannot be explained without demonology' [Trans.].

20 Hans Moravec, *Robot: From Mere Machine to Transcendent Mind* (Oxford: Oxford University Press, 1999), p. 134.

21 Ibid., p. 133.

At the end of this – more pataphysical than metaphysical – tragedy, what Victor Hugo saw as the 'this-will-replace-that' of Progress would end, then, with the predictable arrival of new generations of intelligent machines capable of reproducing themselves: machines which, having long served as our toys, would now be able to toy with us.

This would be the much-heralded *autonomy* of the new bio-ethical thinking and our eminent experts would simply have the task of preparing the human race, with due solicitude, for its inevitable disappearance.

A final throwing-in of the towel sadly reminiscent of *Mind at the End of its Tether*, the literary testament drafted by H.G. Wells shortly before his death not long after Hiroshima. The famous science-fiction author felt that the sciences had taken a hundred-year lead over ordinary thinking, a gap which would continue to grow: 'We pass into the harsh glare of hitherto incredible novelty. It beats the searching imagination. The more it strives, the less it grasps. The more strenuous the analysis, the more inescapable the sense of mental defeat.' The 'intelligent observer', he said, had come to 'the realization that the human story has already come to an end and that *Homo sapiens* . . . is in his present form played out.'[22]

'Progress strikes forward!' claimed Hugo. But not any longer! It has caught up with us and overtaken us, as the history of the twentieth century, with *its mass production of corpses*, has proved.

A black hole of Progress into which has now fallen this whole **philanoia**, this love of madness on the part of the

22   H.G. Wells, *Mind at the End of its Tether* (London/Toronto: William Heinemann, 1945), p. 9, p.18.

sciences and technologies, which is now seeking to organize the self-extermination of a species that is too slow.

But let us listen to the Soviet poet Joseph Brodsky, who knew what he was talking about: 'By its fullness, the future is propaganda.'

If, as they say, *the future torments man*, it is from this congenital burden that the ideology of a totalitarian Progress aspired preventively to liberate Humanity, willingly or otherwise.

For scientific totalitarianism the future is propaganda because propaganda is *propaganda fide* – the propagation of the faith[23] – and progress is merely a *mystical displacement* – the frantic deployment of a force *of physical repulsion and expulsion of man* out of that *divine Creation* which had up until then been for him, the world over, *the beginning of all reality*.

To progress would be to accelerate!

After the break with the geocentrism of Ptolemy and the Copernican delocalization of the 'eternal truths', we would see the exponential development of techno-industrial arsenals giving priority to artillery and explosives, but also to horology, optics, mechanics . . . all things necessary for the elimination of the present world.

The acceleration of a *dromological history* and its rush not now towards the **utopia**, but the **uchronia**, of human time.

After the *century of the Enlightenment*, there would be the century of the *speed of light* and soon, our own century – the century of the *light of speed*.[24]

---

23 I.e. faith in technology and science.
24 Paul Virilio, *L'Horizon négatif* (Paris: Galilée, 1984).

'Three hundred years of diastole, and then came the swift and unexpected systole, like the closing of a fist.'[25]

As we knew already, *speed is the old age of the World*. Subjected to its nihilism, the World retracts, it is *foreclosed*, out of time in the strictest sense.

No need for stereoscopic vision any longer. Before us the film stops rolling; time is no longer, for humanity, a dimension in which it can operate.

With no future – no propaganda any longer, and hence no **faith** – we are suffering from the new *mal du siècle*, depression, the psychoanalysts now tell us. Though they, too, have been *left behind*: 'There is no faith in God any longer, no faith in analysis, no faith in anything!'[26]

*

'I'm as fond of my body as anyone, but if I can be 200 with a body of silicon, I'll take it.' The author of these optimistic remarks is not some kind of advertising man, but a distinguished scientist called Danny Hillis who, we are told, *takes a long view*.[27]

Promises of exceptional longevity, of eternal youth, if not indeed eternal life – the techno-scientific imagination still clings, then, to the strictest biblical orthodoxy, repeating word for word the promise made by Lucifer to the woman the

---

25 H.G. Wells, *The War in the Air*, p. 347.

26 Élisabeth Roudinesco, *Pourquoi la psychanalyse?* (Paris: Fayard, 2000).

27 Danny Hillis, co-founder of the Thinking Machines Corporation, is also the creator of the Long Now Foundation, which is working on a clock designed to function for 10,000 years.

Judaeo-Christian tradition has always associated with 'knowledge': 'Thou shalt not die!'

And why not, indeed, since, after biological man, there would be *virtual man* – an individual who, after living, thinking and acting as though 'he alone had an existence and his fellows were merely vain shadows, pure phantoms', would be invited to become, in his turn, the *shadow of himself*.

And this would justify the claims of the spin doctors, who cannot be accused of excessive originality since, according to them, there is only one way of escaping the new uchronism of human time – without turning your nose up at Progress – and that is no longer to be human – to resort, all in all, to *a substitute immortality*.

And how, indeed, could we fail to notice the pressures of all kinds exerted in these last decades on the human body as such?

'Scientific' pressures to which our lawmakers are constantly adding. In France there was the Caillavet law of 1976, allowing the removal of organs. In 1982 came the '*in vitro* fertilization' affair, followed by all the hype around medically assisted procreation. The law of 20 December 1988 permitted scientific experimentation on volunteers. In May 2001 the vote on the revision of the Veil law, which had now lapsed, took place. A revision which enabled the authorization to sterilize persons termed 'mentally handicapped' to be discreetly included in the provisions. And this at the very point when some people were advocating the reform of psychiatric hospitals, and pointing out that 'no one can regard themselves as immune from mental disorders and depression, which now affect one French person in four'.

Yet, as the humorist Popeck keeps on repeating, 'We are not savages'!

Did not our Republican legislature, which until recently arrogated to itself the barbaric right to deal death to its citizens – and even violent death – abolish the scandal of capital punishment in 1981? And has it not recently abolished *les servitudes militaires*,[28] not to mention introducing the new idea of zero-death wars for our soldiers?

And, still in this same civilizing vein, have not those who govern us promised us painless births and very peaceful deaths in the near future?

'And for pity's sake,' objected Bernard Kouchner, the French Minister of State for Health, indignantly, 'let's not use the term euthanasia, that horrible word which I reject.'[29]

'We are being killed with kindness', as the 80,000 or so Inuits surviving in Eastern Canada are fond of repeating. . . .

And how can we also forget Hitler's private remarks to Hermann Rauschning, author of *The Revolution of Nihilism*. After arguing that biological politics [*Biopolitik*] encompasses the whole of human knowledge of the laws of nature and life, he says: 'If you ask me what I mean by depopulation, I mean the removal of entire racial units. And that is what I intend to carry out – that, roughly, is my task. . . . There are many ways, systematic and comparatively painless, or at any rate bloodless, of causing undesirable races to die out.'[30]

---

28 The reference is not to 'servitudes militaires' in the technical sense, but, in an allusion to Vigny's *Grandeurs et servitudes militaires*, to the abolition of military service. [Trans.]

29 At the point when Holland was legalizing euthanasia, there appeared in *Match* magazine of 21 April 2001 an interview with the singer Dave, entitled 'J'ai aidé ma mère a mourir' [I helped my mother to die], followed by a review of the situation in France by Bernard Kouchner and Florence Portes.

30 See Paul Virilio, 'Le devoir de dépeupler', *Traverses*, January 1985. The passage quoted is from Hermann Rauschning, *Hitler Speaks. A*

The question today, then, is whether the world's populations are not close to having done with soft sciences and technologies, which still take into account the preservation of the planet and its inhabitants; whether they are not now in danger of being swept away by the terrorist excesses of a Laputian *ratio*, a universal **philanoia** attacking a human species which has become 'undesirable' in its entirety, the scandal of an Earth which is, so far as we know, the only biosphere in the solar system.[31]

Scientific integrism's irresistible mystical regression towards the Big Bang of the creation of the universe seems to spare neither the luxuriance of a living world nor the insubordination of those things that are born and die in an unending time, representing so many potential sources of breakdown for the great totalitarian causes *which are linked to a kind of chain of fatality that eliminates Man from the human race* (Charles Alexis de Tocqueville).

To wipe out the human being as such and, with it, the affront of an experimentation which remains a gamble, a series of gambles, and even a Russian roulette scoffing at scientific infallibility. From the solitary nineteenth-century biologist inoculating himself, at his own risk, with the vaccine he has concocted, right down to the determination of the physicists testing out their atom bomb at Trinity Site on

Series of Political Conversations with Adolf Hitler on his Real Aims (London: Thornton Butterworth Ltd, 1939), p. 140.

31 See *Travels into Several Remote Nations of the World in Four Parts by Lemuel Gulliver* (London: Benjamin Motte, 1726). In the century of the Enlightenment, Swift depicts the crazy mathematicians of Laputa and the mad scientists of the Grand Academy of Lagado as scientific antiheroes laying waste to their own country and reducing populations to poverty in the name of knowledge. See Jonathan Swift, Gulliver's Travels (Harmondsworth: Penguin, 1967), pp. 223–237.

16 July 1945, closing their minds to the possible dynamics of this first nuclear test and the great number of dangers being run – the danger, for example, of igniting the earth's atmosphere and bringing about a planetary holocaust of which they would be the first victims.[32]

But let us listen to the onanistic words of the physicist Freeman Dyson, commenting on the apotheosis of the first nuclear explosion in history: 'I have felt it myself. The glitter of nuclear weapons. It is irresistible if you come to them as a scientist. To feel it's there in your hands, to release this energy that fuels the stars, to let it do your bidding. To perform these miracles, to lift a million tons of rock into the sky. It is something that gives people an illusion of illimitable power, and it is, in some ways, responsible for all our troubles . . .'.[33]

In the physicist's *destruction set*, the Earth is an already dead star and the accident of Science is one of those things we 'perpetrate simply because we feel that we should not'.[34]

32 An initial calculation by Edward Teller suggested this might occur. However, a revised estimate subsequently brought the chances of a conflagration down to 'a three-in-a-million chance' (Bill Joy, 'Why the future doesn't need us' – *Wired*, April 2000). In this connection, the reader will remember the decision of a handful of scientists, led by Julius Robert Oppenheimer, to disregard military decisions to interrupt the Manhattan Project after the defeat of Nazi Germany, and to continue it until Hiroshima . . . . 'A symbol of man's ignorance of his own intentions and real desires,' as Charles Mopsik was to write.

33 An extract from the documentary *The Day After Trinity*, quoted by Bill Joy, chief scientist of Sun Microsystems, in 'Why the future doesn't need us'.

34 Edgar Allan Poe, 'The Imp of the Perverse' (1850).

2

History is bunk.

In 1917, the automobile magnate Henry Ford brought into operation the first industrial vehicle assembly line – that other *'chain' of fatality* which would soon make it possible to do away with human workers and replace them with robots.[35]

So, in the very year of the triumph of Lenin, champion of nineteenth-century *historical materialism*, Ford was becoming one of the precursors of its technical dysfunctioning.

In this same spirit, the most recent opinion polls tell us that three out of four French people now mistrust politics but, on the other hand, trust scientists to 'oversee the progress of science and respect for ethics'.

And some are even proposing, right now, to organize

35 The French term for a production line is 'une chaîne (de fabrication)' [Trans.].

referendums and a democratization of information to deal with 'the great social issues, such as biotechnology . . .'.

To confuse ethics and information transmission systems is to forget that mass information provides everyone with a 'dystopic vision' of current events, and poses the well-known problem that accompanies the invention and misuse of any technology: 'unintended consequences, a well-known problem . . . and one that is clearly related to Murphy's law – *"Anything that can go wrong, will"*.'[36]

Eluding any precautionary principle, the systems of information transmission have become bombs which keep on exploding in people's minds, generating ever more complex and extensive accidents, creating that 'uncanny identity which always makes it seem that actions are reported before they are performed, *often the mere possibility of an action'*.[37]

'News isn't after, it's before!', asserted the journalist and novelist Gaston Leroux. Like any strategy, the strategy of news and information is not so much statistical as prophetic and apocalyptic. It derives its power from the chaos it creates

36 In 'Why the future does not need us' (a document which can be consulted on the Internet), Bill Joy speculates also on the perverse effects of information technology in the fields of robotics, genetic engineering, and the nanotechnologies. He focuses, in particular, on the *dystopic scenario* enunciated in his 'Manifesto' by Theodore Kaczinski, alias *the Unabomber*, the Berkeley mathematics Ph.D. who, between 1978 and 1995, sent bombs and booby-trapped parcels to scientists, academics, laboratories and airlines in the USA . . . killing three people and wounding a large number. 'In order to get our message before the public with some chance of making a lasting impression, we've had to kill people', wrote this scientific serial killer who, according to the criminologist Eric Hickey, had *no social skills whatever*! [The passage quoted is from the so-called 'Unabomber Manifesto', paragraph 96 (Trans.).]

37 Karl Kraus, *In These Great Times* (Manchester: Carcanet, 1984), p. 76.

in the 'worst of all possible worlds', and in the end it was the illusionist Georges Méliès who demonstrated this most clearly when he shot his newsreels in the studio before the real events happened. For the inventor of cinematic special effects, tomorrow was today – if not, indeed, yesterday.

Begun in the Quattrocento, the century of Gutenberg, this parody of the Progress of knowledge could not, then, have been achieved without the formidable continuum of the constant updating of technical Darwinism. Without the replacement of writing by industrial printing, would *the vulgarization of techno-scientific progress*, so dear to Buffon, have had any kind of future? Doubtless no more than the eighteenth-century gentleman's cabinet of curiosities, were it not for *the curiosities of the black museum of journalism* with which Karl Kraus regaled us in the early part of the twentieth.

For most of its enthusiasts, trusting in Progress would come down to believing in a beyond of **good** and **evil** – not so much that of a late Nietzscheanism, as the **tov** and **ra** of Judaeo-Christian Genesis and its old – more tribal than moral – laws. This would explain the appearance of new popular heroes capable, like the scientific hero, of destroying themselves by spectacularly flouting **any prohibition**, any limit, any law.

From the eighteenth century onwards, these standards would be offered to the credulity of the public by the young industrial press, and the adulation of the masses would go to the revolutionary *abnormality* of a new kind of women and men with, at the top of the hierarchy, the record-breakers in every field: sportsmen, explorers, soldiers, adventurers, engineers, sailors – all those who would make the front page of the tabloids by showing themselves capable of extreme performances.

Lumped in with these transgression-lovers of all kinds, other outlandish creatures would achieve this ominous fame. Serial killers, 'rippers', poisoners, train or bank robbers, gangsters seeking notoriety in bloody deeds.

As witnesses to the teratological production of their time, Fritz Lang with *M* (1931) and *Doctor Mabuse* (1922), or Bertolt Brecht with his *Threepenny Opera* in 1928 and, later, *The Resistible Rise of Arturo Ui*, informed us of the conflation that was taking place between the anonymous world of organized crime and politics, between the scientist and the terrorist.

From the past exploits of the old *Carbonari* to the crimes of the Brownshirts, from Kropotkin to Jules Joseph Bonnot, Al Capone, Ernst Röhm or Mengele, the industrial mass media progressively inoculated the world with the disease of excess – the nihilism of the gratuitous criminal act making a smooth transition from the *popularity* of the news item to the *populism* of totalitarian propaganda.

The beginnings not so much of the end of history as of a history as bunk – the first fruits of the self-dissolution of a species in which, as Hannah Arendt feared, the **exterminator** would supplant the **predator**.

From the celebrated '*anything goes*' of the old anarchists to that of the totalitarian regimes of the twentieth century, turning to good effect the tried-and-tested methods of the mass media, with *coups d'état* based more on the news media than on military force, and an investigative, incriminatory journalism transformed into a secret police – 'How many people know that it is actually the enemy that is marching at their head?', asked Bertolt Brecht.

But how could they know? In the 1930s, Pierre Mac Orlan had already noted: 'In principle, Hitler does not exist. He is merely a sentimental creation of the crowds.'

The creation of millions of deluded people, or of Dr Joseph Goebbels alone? A former journalist, a man of radio and cinema become Minister of Propaganda and Information for the Third Reich, but also undeniably the precursor of those discreet communications advisers who nowadays keep themselves off-camera, like so many clandestine funeral directors for humanity.

From the glory of the ancient potentates cast in the bronze of the great battles of the past to death on 'live' global TV, the totalitarian systems have — thanks to the mass media — acquired a *replacement rate* considerably more startling than that discerned as early as 1945 by Hannah Arendt.[38]

From the great military decimations to the secret genocides of the Gulag or the extermination camps, from the mass killers of retro-colonialism — in Latin America, Cambodia and Africa — to the exhibitionism of a total terrorist war, the collective murder and ritual sacrifice of the innocents would no longer be hidden activities but unavoidable daily spectacles.

Has the **prohibition to prohibit** — the basic law of techno-scientific progress — become the only law of a lawless globalism?

When, today, European jurists report a massive increase in civil and international litigation, does this come, as they claim with laughable optimism, from an awakening of the legal

38 'Nothing is more characteristic of the totalitarian movements . . . than the startling swiftness with which they are forgotten and the startling ease with which they can be replaced,' wrote ·Hannah Arendt in *The Origins of Totalitarianism* (London, André Deutsch, 1986), p. 305.

awareness of the masses or, rather, from their permanent confrontation with unknown forces whose next victims they fear they may, sooner or later, become?

Not liberation, but global takeover of humanity by totalitarian multimedia powers, applying intensively to populations that age-old strategy which consists in sowing division everywhere – between peoples, regions, towns, countries, races, religions, sexes, generations, and even within families.[39]

As Bertolt Brecht sensed once again: 'They send the looted out looting. The undertaking is a superhuman one; the use of violence, rather than concentrating forces, divides them: *what was elementarily human, too compressed, explodes*. Fragments fly in all directions, and total destruction follows.'

---

39 Wang Xuanming, *The Thirty-Six Stratagems: Secret Art of War* (San Francisco: China Books and Periodicals, 1992).

3

Every system of information – whatever it may
be – is dangerous in the extreme. Even if it is
used for something trivial, it can subsequently be
used for a matter of vital importance

ISAAC ASIMOV

After the American Beat generation of the 1950s, there would,
as the Vietnam war was raging, be Woodstock, the rediscovered
innocence of the hippies, the youthful dream of a return to an
Edenic state finding embodiment in that utopian moral revolution of the 1960s, when 'the limits of the forbidden would
shatter, together with bourgeois morality's dilemma between
what was permitted and what was not' (Alain Ehrenberg).

Providing the opportunity, above all, for the virtual multimedia worlds to edge out the factual world of political
propaganda.

It was indeed in 1968 that that underrated engine of
destruction, television advertising, began in France on the
first national channel. And it was in 1966 that the British

music stations, such as Radio Caroline, first hoisted the Jolly Roger in the free waters off England's shores.[40]

We know the history of this pseudo-liberation of the waves by music, which was to end with the systematic stifling of hundreds of neighbourhood and community radio stations – not, in this case, through state monopoly, but largely as an effect of the monopolies of the commercial media.

Having become, in a few short decades, the cultural agents of 'social modernization', the advertisers would soon be able to announce: 'We do not promote products, we create behaviour.'

They will in fact create campaigns aimed at *parents of both sexes*, and it will be they who will impose on anyone and everyone the new **tablets of the law** – the tablets of the 'beyond **good** and **evil**' of techno-scientific depopulation, leading, as it did, to the immense misery of a mass ego-sexuality and, particularly, to *that shortage on the matrimonial market* announced in 2001 by the researchers of the French national demographic institute (INED) who point out, for illustrative purposes, that in the United States, thirty million American women are single, 33 per cent more than fifteen years ago.[41]

From the 1960s onwards, while the traditional political

---

40 Radio Caroline was located on board an old cargo vessel. More an offshore than a 'pirate' radio-station, it established the use of zones outside national jurisdiction in international waters.

41 'Overthrow virtue'. . . . The consumer society will simply reinvent another 'Ship of Fools' with its 'new values', which are merely *the old ones turned upside down*, a staging of the transgression of the deadly sins – greed, hatred, violence, envy, gluttony, sex, murder – gradually becoming the rules of conduct of a period unaware of the dangers it harbours within itself.

parties and trade unions were endlessly splitting and collaps-
ing, movements like American 'Women's Lib' (which, from
the outset, stood shoulder to shoulder with the civil rights
struggle) or the MLF in France were gaining legitimate emancipation and equal rights, thanks to theatrical actions given
extensive coverage by the new mass media.

The feminist slogans of the 1970s, such as 'The womb is
ours' or 'The production of life belongs to us', gave way in the
1980s to the debasement of these watchwords for purposes of
advertising. **Unisex**. **United Colors** . . . a mix and match of
sexes, generations, races and religions. The child would become
the father of the adult; women, now equipped with penises,
would cease to be the future of man;[42] men would marry men,
and brothers would impregnate their sisters . . . .[43]

'Is the press a messenger? No, it is the event itself. A
speech? No, life itself!' wrote Karl Kraus prophetically.[44]

When advertising in all its forms aspires to provide the entire
terrain of social reality, one can understand why the judiciary, in
its turn, distances itself from the political sphere, and from a
democracy presumed to be the guardian of the old moral
order – to seek out, as we have seen it doing, a new popular
legitimacy based on its tacit alliance with the mass media.[45]

---

42 A reference to Louis Aragon's line, 'L'avenir de l'homme est la
    femme' (*Le Fou d'Elsa*) [Trans.].
43 Between 1982 and 2000, Oliviero Toscani, a man who claimed
    that his campaigns were 'manifestos' which would change mental-
    ities, was one of the undisputed masters of advertising terrorism.
44 Kraus, *In These Great Times*, pp. 75–6.
45 Marie-Anne Frison-Roche and Hubert Haenel, *Les juges et le poli-
    tique* (Paris: PUF, 2001). [It must be remembered here that the
    juge d'instruction, who is responsible for overseeing the investigation
    of crime, is in the French system a member of the judiciary
    (Trans.).]

It will then be under twofold – judicial and multimedia – pressure that the Republican legislators will see themselves forced to undertake the biopolitical conditioning of populations more disarmed than consenting – with the emancipation, in particular, of the child-citizen here copying the well-known emancipation of the child-consumer of merchandising.

From 2001 onwards, children will, for example, be able to reject their patronymic and choose their 'family' name for themselves. There is talk of further reducing the age of majority, which has already happened in practice for those who pursue the profession of fashion model, while underage girls no longer need their parents' agreement to have abortions, and the government advises parliamentarians to avoid passing liberticidal laws which would run the risk 'of making deputies unpopular with young people'.

The legendary times when, as Joseph Roth put it, 'we still believed a republic was a republic' are coming to an end.

In this regard, the election of Silvio Berlusconi as head of the Italian government in 2001 has opened up a *transpolitical era* of a new kind. After his failed try-out of 1994, 'Il Cavaliero' has in fact just carried out a *coup d'état*, and Italy has just toppled over into a two-party system of the third kind in which the alternative is no longer between classical Left and Right, but between politics and the media.

No longer content with occupying the stage of daily life with its great ('Big Brother'-style) game-shows, *telereality* is now invading the sets of the **Res publica**. And for the first time in Europe we are looking on, mesmerized, at the unprecedented victory of the champion of *telecracy* over representative democracy's man, the triumph of audience ratings over universal suffrage.

After the era of the standardization of products and manners of the industrial consumer society comes the era of the synchronization of opinion – the age of an information revolution in which parliamentary geopolitics suddenly gives way to a *chronopolitics* of instantaneity, that 'live' coverage of which television possesses the knack, with the rise of a genuine virtual democracy – that is to say, a *ludic* democracy for infantilized tele-citizens – still to come.

At that point, the political imagination would find itself outstripped once and for all or, more exactly, outpaced (in real time) by the public image of a system of conditioning in which the *optically correct* would succeed the *politically correct* – the vestiges of the ancient deliberative democracy of assemblies of citizens disappearing at the same time as script gives way to the screen.

In fact, this decline of the republican ritual of election in favour of a mere emission/reception of more or less subliminal messages will be further aggravated by all those who are now doing their utmost to proclaim the merits of future on-line electronic democracy using the Internet. After the television screen, it is the computer screen which is now drumming out this slogan: '**E-democracy** *is on the way, have your say and help to shape the public debate.*'

And to justify this, the new cyberculture enthusiasts assert that 'we are moving from an intermittent democracy, with periodic elections, to a *continuous democracy*', in which citizenship would be boiled down, all in all, to its simplest expression: that of making a forecast.

An anecdote to illustrate this diversion: for a while now, **Johann** has been presenting the stock-market results on a German Internet site. But **Johann** does not exist. He is the first virtual presenter of the electronic era, which is one way of bringing sacrificial pawns into the electro-economic fiction of the global casino, that great planetary deregulation in which *those who have most success are those who do the least thinking* (Abby Cohen).

But let us not forget the tied result of the American elections of November 2000, when some of the media offered to resort to the live broadcasting of a *hand of poker* as a way of settling the contest between the presidential candidates. In this way, the contradictory calculations of a defective electoral system would give way to the mathematics of chance, and wearisome political broadcasts would be shifted into the – eminently more profitable – category of light entertainment and game-shows.

And why not, since – as Norman Mailer explained at the time – 'Since the Watergate affair, the media think they can get away with anything'. And American politicians seem to have forgotten Asimov's precious recommendation, that old classic of intelligence-gathering: 'Every system of the transmission of information, whatever it may be, is dangerous in the extreme . . . . The government is not keen for a transmission system to remain infallible, unless it is put under its control.'

Might democracy be perishing from the breakdown of its own information systems, the bug in the instrument of governmental transmission?

Eight months after the dubious American ballot of 2000, a report by the presidents of the Massachusetts Institute of Technology and the California Institute of Technology revealed that between four and six million votes had gone uncounted, while George W. Bush had ultimately been elected with a lead of 537 votes over the Democrat Al Gore.

Like the Internet's **Johann**, between four and six million American voters had virtually ceased to exist, and the authors of the report concluded that they would continue to 'have legitimate concerns about embarking on another presidential election'.[46]

And, to make the point even better, at the moment when, with much use of high-tech advertising, they were exhuming Nietzsche's superman, the world's most powerful head of state was turned into a kind of endangered political mutant in that series of films shot shortly before the presidential elections of 2000 in which Bill Clinton appeared washing his car, cooking or taking a snooze in the famous Oval Office – thereby demonstrating that the tenant of the White House was no longer thought to serve much of a purpose.[47]

And why tire yourself when everything runs without human intervention, when it has even been suggested that strikes against rogue states hostile to American interests might be automated, and when missiles are quite capable of finding their destinations by themselves?

But this was nothing as yet. Invulnerable America was subsequently to get a *part-time president*, George Jnr. Seven months into his term, he had spent half that time in the country, on his Texas ranch or at Camp David, the presidential holiday residence, or at his parents' home . . . just before the Pentagon and the World Trade Center exploded.

---

46 The report was written by David Baltimore and Charles Vest, presidents respectively of Caltech and MIT [Trans.].
47 The videos in question were shot for the White House Correspondents' Association Dinner of April 29 2000 [Trans.].

'Intelligence which relies on high technology, on electronic eavesdropping and satellites is all very well, but we cannot hit the terrorists if we don't have human information,' concluded General Norman Schwartzkopf at the time.

Echoing the comments of the father of cybernetics: 'No, the future offers very little hope for those who expect that our new mechanical slaves will offer us a world in which we may rest from thinking.'[48]

48 Wiener, *God & Golem, Inc.*, p. 69.

4

Of the devoted priests of power,
there are many who regard with
impatience the limits of mankind.[49]

NORBERT WIENER

'For many years all armies have played war games, and these
games have always been behind the times. It has been said
that in every war, the good generals fight the last war, the bad
ones the war before the last. That is, the rules of the war
game never catch up with the facts of the real situation,' wrote
Norbert Wiener in 1964.[50]

We are always one war behind, and just as there are no experts
in atomic warfare (a war in which the adversaries would have
possessed a bomb and used it), there are not yet any experts
in global terrorist warfare, even among the terrorists.

When, on September 12 2001 – after the unprecedented

---

49 Wiener, *God and Golem, Inc.* p. 53.
50 Ibid., p. 60.

series of attacks perpetrated on the Pentagon and the World Trade Center – George W. Bush declared that his country was the champion of **good**, and that the battle against terrorism would be 'a monumental struggle of **good** versus **evil**', and '**good** will prevail',[51] he was speaking the same language as his father in 1991, itself copied from the language of the 'just war' fought by the United States against Nazism half a century before!

A language that is all the more difficult to speak as, since the collapse of the USSR, America's new world hegemony has mainly made itself felt by an arrogance based on its crushing technical superiority rather than on its elevated morality.

But let us remember that when, at Casablanca in January 1943, President Roosevelt declared the first total war in history, the aim was not simply to inflict massive physiological and material destruction on the German nation, but to demolish *its spiritual front*.

Let us further remember that when he was close to being routed, Hitler riposted with the famous *telegram 71* – 'If the war is lost, let the nation perish!' – by which, before his suicide, he resolved to combine his efforts with those of his opponents to complete the extermination of his own people by wiping out the resources of its habitat – its reserves of food, fuel and drinking water . . . if not, indeed, to resort to gas to rid himself of them.[52]

---

51 'This will be a monumental struggle of good versus evil. But good will prevail' (Office of the [White House] Press Secretary, 'Remarks by the President in Photo Opportunity with the National Security Team', 12 September, 2001) [Trans.].

52 Paul Virilio, 'L'État suicidaire', *Insécurité du territoire* (Paris: Stock, 1976).

After the crash of the *Net economy* in 2000 and the crash in 2001 of the Pentagon's 'Net strategy', brought about by a handful of crazed suicide attackers, we find ourselves, in fact, facing an unprecedented situation, since it is one which is *globally suicidal*.

If Minister Paul Henri Spaak congratulated himself, during the era of nuclear deterrence, on the existence of a *balance of nuclear terror* that enabled war between the two great blocs to be avoided, how do things stand with this today, when the ego-mysticism of the one side can no longer be distinguished from the techno-scientific mysticism of the others – all united beyond **good** and **evil** by the inauthenticity now shared by broadcasters in both East and West, and by those watched by Muslim TV viewers?

A global suicidal state – a loss of the instinct of self-preservation. Of the self and the species. When, on 14 September 2001, President George W. Bush ordered 'a day of prayer and remembrance', how were we to forget that since his election seven months before, his only previous television appearance had been to defend American policy on the commercialization of human embryos, to incite humans to take that great anthropological step 'in which, for the first time in their history', they would 'produce human beings in order to destroy them'?

As we know, the multilateral damage caused currently by an optics which has become global would have been impossible without the *policing of the stars* by the spy satellites of the nuclear status quo, that ever greater sophistication of technical perception which was to lead to the – no longer natural, but artificial – selection of the ocular imagery of man. An audiovisual derealization as a result of which the worldly public, unlike the sceptical Thomas, would end up believing what it would not touch and could not have 'seen'.[53]

Humanity's escape from its congenital incompleteness, from the dissatisfaction with being oneself, would no longer seem to be through the psychoanalyst's 'illicit science of souls' or the abrogation of the old prohibitions. On the other hand, when Cioran wrote that *to live is to blind oneself to one's own dimensions*, he was stating better than anyone the ultimate response furnished by Progress to what has remained a permanent metaphysical demand – to Nietzsche's stirring 'Here I am, I can do no other.'[54]

The new image strategies have taken care of this, since, for the ordinary run of mortals, *to know how things appear* is the least of our worries. What does it matter that the appearances of the world find themselves reduced to fleeting optical illusions, provided that the screen – here following the windscreen – relieves everyone of the exact measure of their smallness.[55]

It is not by chance, then, that, in parallel with the sophistication of technical perception, we are seeing a decline in the use of high-tech equipment for utilitarian purposes, and the recent rerouting of that equipment to religious, paraphilosophical, transpolitical and syncretic ends . . . . The immediacy, ubiquity and omniscience of the monitors and terminals of domestic computers finally taking over the task of

53 As the attack on the World Trade Center was being broadcast live, many TV viewers believed they were watching one of those disaster movies which proliferate endlessly on our TV screens. It was by switching channels and finding the same pictures on all the stations that they finally understood that 'it was true'!

54 I have not been able to trace this quotation. However, there is a clear reference here on Nietzsche's part to Luther's famous phrase: 'Hier steh' ich, ich kann nicht anders' [Trans.].

55 Here I have adapted a phrase of Schlegel's.

putting back in place the dubious methods everyone employs to assert their *dependence on what sets them outside themselves*.

On what, for rare moments, seems to render bodies insubstantial – dreams, trances, hypnosis, orgasms, alcohol, stimulants. . . .

And among these age-old techniques of self-disappropriation – images, words, these inflexible powers, *capable of preventing us from living, and from living in our place* (Alfred Döblin).

One could read recently, for example, in a French regional newspaper, this death notice in which the Buddhist 'vehicle' is likened to the vehicles of space conquest, or of Star Trek: 'X . . ., that little cosmonaut, has decided to change mission and his face shows us he has awakened to his Buddha-nature and will be able to be reborn in better conditions. . .'.

Elsewhere, we find computer specialists wanting, in the best Rabbinical tradition, to call their computer GOLEM 1, whereas some Wall Street traders, still traumatized by the computer crash of 1987, hired voodoo priestesses 'to cleanse their sites of evil forces'.

While some fundamentalists refuse to allow the bodies of Internet users into their cemeteries, *tribute websites for the dead* are opening which enable the families of grieving Internet users to pay their respects to their dear departed, without any need to travel.

Without travelling, either, the thirty-nine members of the American 'Heaven's Gate' cybersect believed when they committed suicide that they would meet up again instantaneously, with all their worldly goods and chattels, at the gates of Paradise, in the hereafter of their computer screens. . . .

Here, communication techniques do not in any way enable anyone to 'communicate'. They merely have a *compensatory function*, sparing each person the painful 'encounter of the self with itself' which still trammels the consciousness of every human being.[56]

What has not ceased to prosper inordinately in the world, over these centuries of Progress which have seethed with ideologies, utopias, delusions, false trails and bluff of all kinds (now consigned to the cupboard of lost illusions), is, ultimately, that *imposture of immediacy* discerned in tragic times by Dietrich Bonhoeffer – this technical elaboration of a *false proximity* imitating the *dilectio proximi* of the theologian to the point where one can hardly tell the difference between the two.

In the words of the old adage, to live is 'to be among men' [*inter homines esse*]. What the high priests of techno-scientific Progress have striven to destroy is this preference for the near and the neighbour which established the heterogeneity of our consciousness, replacing it with the fearsome 'misknow thyself' contemned by Kafka.

At the beginning of our era, Saint Augustine, long held in thrall by spectacles and shows, observed: 'One sees oneself in those who seem transported by such objects, one soon becomes *a secret actor in the tragedy.*'

Bossuet, following many others, will remark that in theatres the dangerous nature of the spectacle is further increased by the collective emotion, that the air is more harmful there than elsewhere.

---

56 'Conscience appears as an afterthought' (Hannah Arendt, 'Thinking and Moral Considerations: A Lecture', *Social Research*, no. 38/3, Fall 1970, p. 444). In this lecture, Arendt inquires into her contemporaries' 'curious, quite inauthentic inability to think' (p. 417).

And how can we forget the impressions of a Pierre Mac Orlan moving in 1932 through the chaos of Berlin with all its parades – of Hitler, the *Stahlfront*, the *Hammer and Sickle*? On 13 March, the writer entered the Sportpalast, transformed for the occasion into a red cathedral. There were thirty thousand spectators there, Mac Orlan tells us: 'The clamour is the clamour you hear at the six-day cycle races when the pack takes off in pursuit of bonuses. It is also the fearsome elemental clamour of the boxing halls, when one of the fighters is "taking a hammering".'[57]

And the writer notes that he is gradually becoming insubstantial, dissolving, losing his personality: 'It is an extraordinary feeling which is difficult to analyse since it is more physical than cerebral.'

After the resounding failures of the (military, political, nationalistic, etc.) totalitarianisms of the nineteenth and twentieth centuries, which exploited to the full the mystical fusion/confusion of each individual's body with the extravagant, super-potent fusions/confusions of a common body (the army, the masses, the body politic, etc.), which did their living and thinking for them, and withdrew from the creative physiological dimension in a manner worthy of a Thomas Hobbes, individual incompleteness is now dependent on *simulators of proximity* (**TV, the Web, mobile phones**) as highly effective as flight-, weapons- or driving-simulators, drawing, in this case, on an *imposture of immediacy* that is more dystopian than ever.

After the primitive simulators, such as the Lumière broth-

---

57 Pierre Mac Orlan, *L'Allemagne en sursis* (Paris: UGE, 1984).

ers' 'candid camera' – unveiling the private lives of its inventors – global cinema newsreels, Anglo-Saxon documentarism, Italian neo-realism or the vogue for pornography and so on, we have arrived today at 'reality television', such as the famous 'Big Brother', combining *all the existing media of communication* – for example, in France, terrestrial television (M6), satellite broadcasting (Canal 27 on TPS[58]) and the Internet, the telephone system and SMS (short message service) for voting.

If we add that this type of programme – *claiming to show real life and democratize the star system* – has existed for many years, both in Europe and the Antipodes, in Germany and Thailand or Paraguay, we can easily understand that the *experimental subjects* are not the volunteers locked away here or there in the enforced intimacy of the lofts, but the millions of *secret actors* engaged, without knowing it, in the first episodes of a formidable role-playing game in which all fashionable TV viewers are trained to scrutinize, to react, and virtually to eliminate '*that other world which is man*'.[59]

Let us make no mistake about it, the modernity of 'Big Brother' and its clones is the direct successor to the multimedia presentation of the Gulf and Kosovo conflicts . . . an image strategy which preceded the perfectly orchestrated image strategy of the terrorist attacks of September 2001.

'No result, pathetic failure, political aberration . . .' they

---

58 In France, the highly successful 'Loft Story' reality show was broadcast daily 22 hours out of 24 on Canal 27 [Trans.].

59 François Rabelais, *The Histories of Gargantua and Pantagruel* (London: Penguin, 1955), p. 195: 'Then scrupulously peruse, the books of the Greek, Arabian, and Latin doctors once more, not omitting the Talmudists and Cabalists, and by frequent dissections gain a perfect knowledge of that other world which is man.'

said ten years ago of a *commerce de guerre* which no longer seemed to profit anyone and which, in fact, ruined national entities one after the other, disrupted democratic armies and destroyed diplomatic, political, economic and social fabrics . . . .

And yet the highly media-conscious Tony Blair had warned us in 1999, at the beginning of the lamentable Kosovo War: 'This is a new kind of war, not for a territory but for *universal values*.'

In effect, that war was no longer a specifically 'military' one. In it the NATO forces were reduced to a few groups of specialists, mere executants of (or executioners in) techno-scientific operations of destruction.[60] *A war with zero deaths* for professionals who would no longer die on the field of honour, but perish discreetly, in a manner belonging more properly to epidemiology or to industrial accidents.

While on the ground, terroristic, marginal armed bands dispersed – Serbian, Albanian, Kosovar or others – charged with doing the *dirty work* in a 'war' which regressed towards the anomie of tribal massacres, pillage, hostage-taking, racketeering and terroristic trafficking of all kinds.

Unprecedentedly, during the Kosovo conflict, the two officially declared enemies were never to meet physically anywhere, thus marking *the disappearance of a real battlefield* of a kind which still existed, in a latent state, during the Falklands/Malvinas and Gulf conflicts.

In this way, the risks of fraternization between combatants, as well as any true proximity, were eliminated

---

60 See Paul Virilio, 'Une science à grand spectacle', *Le Monde diplomatique*, July–August 2001. See also Virilio, *Strategy of Deception* (London: Verso, 2000) on the Kosovo conflict and, particularly, on the cybernetic capacities of massive information.

automatically, to the advantage of a global information system freed of any concern for verisimilitude . . . of anything elementarily human.

As we were to observe two years later in New York, this lesson would rapidly be assimilated by the new strategists of world terrorism. There would no longer be any heroes, star performers, demands or military operators, and the actions undertaken would be perceived, like any natural catastrophe, as '**manifestations of divine anger**'.

5

The great technological events may change
our lives but they will not create a new
form of art. They may create a generation of art
critics who will tell us, 'This is art!'

ORSON WELLES

'The world [is going] to ruin,' warned Karl Kraus, and 'man's
feeling of superiority triumphs in the expectation of a spectacle
to which only contemporaries are admitted.'[61] Like
Stockhausen, the grand old master of electronic music, flying
into raptures over the spectacle of the New York attacks which
killed four thousand people in September 2001: 'What we have
witnessed is the greatest work of art there has ever been!'[62]

61 Kraus, *In These Great Times*, p. 57.
62 In translating this passage, I have followed contemporary German
    newspaper reports of Stockhausen's comments ['*das grösste
    Kunstwerk, das es je gegeben hat*']. These do, however, seem to repre-
    sent a somewhat questionable account both of the composer's actual
    words and of the context [Trans.].

Why not four million dead next time? Deterring art from being the manifestation of bodies can lead us a long way – to the era of the atom, of biological fiction, of avatars and televisual terrorism.

And this is indeed the paradox of a 'culture mill' which has, since the nineteenth century, hitched itself to the invention of that *consanguinity of man and instrument* (Gabriele d'Annunzio) that will dictate what is or is not modern or revolutionary.

When Lenin writes that 'Communism is the power of the Soviets plus the electrification of the country', one may go beyond the hackneyed formula to think either of the Italian Futurists announcing the advent of the '*multiple man who gets tangled up in iron and feeds on electricity*', or of the Islamist suicide hijackers hurtling their planes into the towers of the World Trade Center.

Similarly, the clear-sighted art lover will wonder how Van Gogh (whom Signac called a 'mad phenomenon') and, after him, the originators of Fauvism, would have painted without the illumination of industrial lighting, whether by gas or electricity, rivalling the brilliance of the regal star of the Mediterranean.

What would the Realist or Naturalist schools of the nineteenth century have been without the objective accident of the photographic pose, or the Bauhaus and Moholy-Nagy without the aerialization of human vision and the cinema? Or German Expressionists without the industrial production of corpses by military-scientific progress – with the 'ghosts'[63] that were to

---

63 In *War and Cinema*, Virilio writes of 'the derealization of a battle in which ghosts played an ever greater role – screen ghosts of enemy pilots served to confirm that they had been shot down, and ghostly radar images, voices and echoes came through on the screens, radios and sonars' (London: Verso, 1989), p. 76 [Trans.].

invade the radar screens of the Battle of Britain in 1940 yet to come, supplanting as they did all other audiovisual warning systems, and hence all other systems for representing coming dangers.

And one will also wonder about the paradoxical logic of Mies van der Rohe asserting that '**less is more**', and the fanaticism of Adolf Loos judging *ornament a crime against modernity* – half a century before Andy Warhol declared: 'If you want to know about Andy Warhol, just look at the surfaces of my paintings. . . . There's nothing behind it', and – talking about himself as though, in principle, he did not exist – 'It's all there. There's nothing missing. I am everything my press album says I am.'

There are many ways of being iconoclastic. You can burn pictures and those who painted them, erase or tamper with the cartouches of monuments, break religious statues or blow up those of political idols, as at the end of the Communist era.

But how is it when the iconoclast is the plastician himself?

After the fall of their traditional patrons (divine-right monarchy, princes, the Church of Rome), artists, in an attempt to survive, to be famous for at least fifteen minutes, had at their disposal neither the panoply of the warrior, the tools of the politician, nor the irrefutability of the scientist.

By contrast with a literature which, by its technical calling, had involved itself at a very early stage in current events, thanks to the talent of its writers of serialized fiction and its journalist-novelists (from Rabelais to Stendhal, Balzac, Dickens, London, Zola and Cendrars), the rest of the culture mill stood aloof, bogged down in an official academic staidness, shamefully conservative.

Yet in 1818, *The Raft of the Medusa*, that great manifesto-painting by Géricault, a man with a liking for the stray news item, penetrated the world of political and judicial affairs to make headlines in the French and Anglo-Saxon press. At the Salon of 1857, in a feverish social context, it would be the turn of Courbet and the *naturalist* scandal. And in 1874, 'Impressionism', invented by a mercenary criticism. . . .[64]

Cheered by this entry into the grand manoeuvres of the world of news technologies, many plasticians saw here a practical source of substitute activity and renewal, both in terms of profit and aesthetically.

'Slow news, no news!' The artists of the twentieth century, like the anarchist with his home-made bombs, the revolutionary suicide bomber or the mass killers celebrated by the mass-circulation press, would themselves become wielders of plastic explosives, visual mischief-makers, anarchists of colour, form and sound, before coming to occupy the gutter press's gallery of horrors.

Soon, as René Gimpel was to remark – or, later, Orson Welles – contemporary art could no longer do without the connivance of *those art critics who would 'tell us: "This is art"',* simply because art had become *unrecognizable.*

And, like the statues of the great Buddhas of Bamiyan after the Taliban had gone by, it would be impossible to identify it unless its authenticity were duly certified by some specialist or appraiser.

As when paper money replaced gold at the beginning of

---

64 The term was coined by the critic Louis Leroy as a derogatory description of Monet's approach in the painting 'Sunrise: Impression' [Trans.].

the last century, it would now be necessary to check out the market prices to learn that in June 2001, for example, a Picasso was worth more than a Monet, or a Warhol more than a Rembrandt – though this is of little consequence on the *global disappearance market*, where telepresence is supplanting the real presence of the art object, and also of its buyer and seller.

*

What are we talking about today when we speak of art? This is a question it has become increasingly difficult to answer.

Art is like a currency which must remain in circulation, claimed a perceptive August Wilhelm Schlegel.

But in a world that is resolutely accidental – that is to say, an enemy to its *own substance* – one wonders what bonds of authenticity can still unite the market value of our art objects to their plastic presence and, above all, what can still bind us to them?

If, according to the time-honoured formula 'art is long and life is short', the uproarious entry of contemporary and 'current' works into the all-powerful news market – where, as we know, merchandise is valueless after twenty-four hours or twenty-four seconds – has destroyed the notion of **durée**, which had until then been involved in the assessment of the object, at the same time as it has destroyed that other tangible quality that was its **rarity** – the fact that the work is considered unique from its conception or has become so over the centuries.

What, at first glance, distinguishes the true work is, as Rainer Maria Rilke wrote, its 'infinite solitude', the enigmatic attraction of a *uniqueness* which, paradoxically, offers the multitude of its sensory adequations to those who, *in look-ing at them, produce half the pictures* (Paul Klee), and often more than that – like that nostalgic emperor of China who com-plained to their creator, Li Ssu-Hsur, about the noise made by the waterfalls he had painted, which were preventing him from sleeping.[65]

The true work of art is not, then, one of those arrange-ments of mirrors in which the magicians of Ancient Greece claimed to re-create the universe for the naive Athenian onlookers, any more than it is, for the creator or the specta-tor, a narcissistic reflection or the product of some 'real-time' dramaturgy.

The work of art is not academic; it conforms to no pre-conceived plan and expresses only *the extreme veneration of receptiveness* or, more trivially, of the extreme vigilance of the living body that sees, hears, intuits, moves, breathes and changes.

'*Life's emotions are basically merely steps*', confided the great dancer Sylvie Guillem. 'I regard my body as an instrument of discovery. . . . You have to astonish yourself each time, to dis-cover yourself.'[66]

Unlike that modern Olympic champion who declared that *his body was his worst enemy*, Sylvie, when she is dancing, makes an ally of hers. 'One day,' she adds, '*I danced without being there*, with *only the memory of my technique*. I have regretted it ever since.'

---

65 François Cheng, *Vide et plein. Le langage pictural chinois* (Paris: Le Seuil, 1979). One thinks, too, of the open systems of Platonic thought and the expression coined by the Greeks, *kalokagathia*, which refers to the beauty and goodness of a consoling art.

66 Sylvie Guillem, 'Mon corps et moi', *Le Nouvel Observateur*, 3 January 1996. 'Avoid over-dancing', she says.

Similarly when, at the beginning of the twentieth century - 'that century of machines', as Picabia called it – Sergei Diaghilev commanded his dancers to 'astonish' him,[67] one might understand him to be saying: 'Don't do it like machines, do it the way you would in real life when you do everything for the first and last time, for if, in real life, time never ends, nothing is repeated either, nothing is exactly banal for us, every moment that arrives is a new moment – the ordinary course of life is the extraordinary, the permanent feature of existence is astonishment.'

'You make a choice every second – that is the magic of life!' confided one beautiful actress, alluding to the old philosopher's forgotten remark, or the words of that lover of nonsense, André Isaac: 'I am always on the brink, on the brink of something.'[68]

And I myself have written: '**Here** is no longer, all is **now**.' All the arts – and particularly the arts of re-presentation – were, then, to be fatally damaged, then destroyed, by the constant acceleration of technologies of presentation and reproduction both dromological and dromoscopic which, by reducing the space and time between subject and object to zero, were to eliminate, as a matter of course, not just the concepts of rarity and *durée*, but *the nodal points of the potentiality and the 'becoming' of the work of art* – its phenomenology.[69]

*

67 He also famously asked Cocteau to do the same [Trans.].
68 André Isaac, alias Pierre Dac (1893–1975), the great mid-twentieth-century French humorist and parodist [Trans.].
69 See Paul Virilio, *The Art of the Motor*, Trans. Julie Rose (Minneapolis: University of Minnesota Press, 1996).

The total eclipse of consciousness of the Trinity Site physicists was, then, culturally avant-garde. It would, in effect, be followed by the eclipse of consciousness on the part of the worldly, joining without too many complaints in the countdown of *the balance of nuclear terror*.

As a continuation of total war by other means, nuclear deterrence marked the end of the distinction between wartime and peacetime, and cleared the way for a *worldwide state of undeclared war* between the Western and Soviet blocs – of which, quite logically, terrorism and gangsterism would be the main beneficiaries.

Similarly, techno-scientific retro-progress having exhausted the interest the inhabitants of the biosphere could still take in their future, it was normal that they should turn away from it to the wasteland of origins. At the beginning of the Cold War, a start was made in the United States on digging trenches in suburban gardens, and storing away in prefabricated shelters all that seemed essential to survive the end of the world in the best of conditions . . . .

The authorities in the big cities had even organized a few evacuation exercises in urban centres, but facts had to be faced: in the event of a general nuclear alert, millions of drivers, fleeing together on overcrowded exit routes, would be caught in inextricable traffic jams, and perish before they reached their suburban bunkers.

The inhabitants of the old European bastion, for their part, adapted as best they could to the Welfare State's mutation into a suicidal one.

The reversed perspective of a planetary life entering its terminal phase would give rise to a conservatism of a kind previously almost unknown, a *museomania* which would far exceed the old academy of the Muses, and would merely reveal the dreadful poverty of Western techno-culture.

There would be museums for everything – in a kind of cult of trash or 'unrecognized pop art', the fetishistic infatuation of ageing populations with all that had been rejected, forgotten, outdated, all that had previously been found wearisome or repellent.

At the point when we were condemned to leave for ever, we would set about collecting, in no particular order, the old mechanical toys, the products and sentimental flotsam of a failed modernity.

Arctophiles and philumenists, collectors of breweriana and even dachshundiana – we would give names to all these devotees, and to their collecting passions. And they would have their various museums to go to: museums of photography, nougat, coffee-pots, the cinematograph, Camembert, marriage, posters, peasant and working-class life, railways, household electrical goods. . . .

Little by little, the differences between the contemporary living-space and the sites of the archaeological past would fade. Modern Europe would take on a discreetly funereal character.

Lost amid their contemporary suburbs, the historic towns and cities – with their palaces, cathedrals and museums – would become like those dead cities of Antiquity, with their tombs and mausoleums, where the weapons, vehicles, treasure, familiar objects and images of the pleasures they had enjoyed would be laid out before the unseeing eyes of the dead.

Before ultimately handing them over to an exotic young crowd, some municipal officials are now proposing to parody the libations and funeral orgies of ancient times there. Like Christophe Girard of the Paris city authority, who announced to the press in April 2001: 'I want to get away from the usual ways of using cultural sites. A museum doesn't have to be a temple. You can dance in the Louvre in front of the Rembrandts, as they have done at the Rijksmuseum in Amsterdam . . . I have set myself the task of restoring the capital's festive character.'[70]

Yet vast tracts were reduced to no-go areas, refugee camps or conservation areas, nature reserves with their moribund fauna and flora.

The mountains, the coast, disused military or industrial sites, worked-out mines, closed-down blast furnaces, the back-to-back housing and tenements of a disappeared proletariat would be listed as historic monuments.

With techno-culture – as flashback or feedback – continuing on its retreat towards the void of origins, the mass media would soon lead with a story of 'Mayan sculpture and Zulu masks to stand alongside the Mona Lisa'.

The time of *primal arts* was the childhood of art, if not indeed its prenatal state.

A museum would be built for it not far from the Eiffel Tower, and the 'scientific adviser' to the enterprise – at the inauguration of the new galleries of primal arts at the Louvre – would be able to tell us: 'There are no longer any grounds for the old quarrel between the so-called aesthetic and the so-called ethnographic approaches.'

Doubtless because, long before playing host to what were

70 'Green, gay and a specialist in the luxury industries, this is the – unprecedented – profile of the new culture spokesman in the Paris *Mairie*' (Interview with Sylvie Santini in *Match*), and 'On peut danser devant les Rembrandt', *Le Journal du dimanche*, 22 April 2001.

called primal arts, the Louvre was no longer anything but a *miroir des limbes*, a huge ethnographic warehouse living on beyond its own end, as André Malraux had predicted, thanks to a considerable pedagogical/commercial effort directed towards the new mass tourism, and also towards a native population for whom its own culture had become, in a few short decades, as alien as that of distant civilizations which disappeared thousands of years ago.

There was, then, really no basis for the quarrel, since 'those who, in looking at them, do half the work of the pictures' (Paul Klee) and those who, by reading them, do half the work of books (Voltaire) had long been marked out for decimation.

Ethnographic museums – above all, *musées des Invalides*.

Here again, we have kept tally of our accursed artists, of the suicide-artists of modernity – the failures, the suicides, the halt and the lame, the alcoholics, the obsessives, the addicts, the insane or the devotees of mutilation or gratuitous crimes – but we have said nothing about the constant aggravation of the ill-treatment inflicted on an equally accursed public – blinded, deafened, despised and, finally, declared the enemy by *arts of sheer terror*.

Yet, in the middle of the fateful 1930s, the author of *Brave New World*, Aldous Huxley, was already concerned at the decline of a European culture in which the stimulation of the senses was coming to mean the organization of ever more violent orgies (sex/blood/race . . .), with the risk that societies in crisis would be pushed into new massacres. He even took the view that these aesthetic problems justified international conferences as urgent as those called to deal with disarmament or the world economy.[71]

71 'The orgies of nationalism are not Platonic orgies-for-orgies'-sake.

And we may well wonder today what poisoned chalice is being offered to a demeaned public when the decision comes down from on high that no distinction is now to be made between the aesthetic and ethnographic approaches to exhibited works; that the field of immediate consciousness will be treated in the same way as things that are necessarily of the order of an instrumentalized knowledge – disembodied and, indeed, far removed from the body.

A bit like Andy Warhol putting his faith, like so many before him, in the inequality created between artists and spectators by the techniques of the advertisers' *high-speed art* and the global public's predisposition to obey the orders and signals of *operative images* . . . .

With *The Mystery of Picasso*, a film made in 1956 by Henri-Georges Clouzot, spectators had already been treated to the unveiling of the genesis of the master's works by the camera.

Readers will remember seeing Picasso behind a great translucent panel where he stood to paint – the panel serving as interface between himself and the lens. As in a children's cartoon, the works that were forming appeared in transparency on this medium, thus giving the viewers the illusion of watching the various phases of their gestation 'live', and ultimately, after the usual rethinking and retouching, of watching these images brought painfully into the world by an exhausted but satisfied creative artist.

They lead to practical results – to the piling up of armaments, to senseless economic competition . . . and ultimately to war.' Huxley, *Beyond the Mexique Bay* (London: Chatto & Windus, 1974), p. 85. Huxley went on to advocate new 'emotional cultures' (ibid., p. 86).

Shortly afterwards, taking advantage of the remarkable progress of echographic techniques, obstetricians would provide the mass media with a bulk supply of the successive images of a foetal life which had until then remained invisible to ordinary mortals.

In *Le Monde des Débats* (September 2000), Jean-Pierre Mohen, the director of the Centre de recherche et de restauration des musées de France, regaled us with the following announcement: 'Radiographic and other studies are providing new and original information on what painters have done, *consciously or otherwise*.'

With this final puzzle, the fusion/confusion of arts and techno-sciences could be said to have reached its end – that long deconstruction begun, consciously or otherwise, by artists themselves some one hundred and fifty years ago!

After the biological parent, the 'creative artist' would, in his turn, be declared suspect, and would have to bow out before the scientist and the infallible 'know-how' of his instruments – before those who now call themselves 'art geneticists' and direct their efforts, using the chemical, physical and electronic arsenals at their disposal, 'to making visible and available to everyone what artists had concealed beneath the surface of their works', whereas before *genetics* (in the sense of the genesis of works of art), 'all we had to go on' in literature, painting and music, they claim, 'was the end result'.[72]

---

72 'Painting belongs essentially to the field of the senses. This is a fact, and all the knowledge in the world will not prevail against the experience of a painter's eye,' declared Jean Bazaine in February 1992, prefacing with these remarks the irreplaceable work of *Nuances*, the journal of the Association pour le respect de l'intégrité du patrimoine artistique (ARIPA).

'Once the painting is finished, I have nothing to say,' explained Balthus not so very long ago. But no matter; the scientist will make him speak, will get the information out of him. It is as though, running Clouzot's film backwards, the prenatal sequences of the work were to resurface in succession.

After the Cartesian animal-machine or the man-machine, here is the automatic work of art dreamt of by Hugo or by Dada, art reduced to the criteria of the optimal play of self-adapting machines by 'scientific experts' ignorant of what the cyberneticist knows: namely, that the machine can become 'more intelligent', but it 'does not learn' and, ultimately, soon ceases to interest or astonish the general public.[73]

It is, perhaps, to soften the blow of this probable disaffection that the new cultural promoters are now trying to substitute the advertising displays of *high-speed art* for techno-scientific explication.

We learn, for example, that a powerful cosmetics multinational recently formed partnerships with the Palazzo Pitti and the Barberini to co-produce art shows and participate in the 'restoration' of old works of art which will, we are told, be *readapted to current tastes*.

Exhibited in this way, after a clean-up and a makeover, the magisterial works of Tintoretto or Titian will be able to convey to the general public and to the students in the schools 'a delightfully effective advertising message, enabling us to divine the pop potential of the masterworks of past art', as was announced by Antonio Paolucci, the superintendent of

---

73 'Orson Welles on TV', *De Visu*, no. 4.

the artistic treasures and historical monuments of the city of Florence.

The works of Raphael and Velasquez have suffered the same *post mortem* attentions at the Prado.

And Jean-Pierre Cuzin, head curator of the department of painting at the Louvre, announced to the press that '*the Mona Lisa which, like Marilyn, draws in the crowds*' will soon have its own separate room donated by the Japanese private television channel NTV which, as we know, has already funded in full the 'restoration' of the ceilings of the Sistine Chapel.

'Drawing copies the residue of a vision,' observed Alberto Giacometti. 'It is my belief, whether we are dealing with painting or sculpture, that only the drawing counts. If one more or less mastered drawing, all the rest would be possible. . . . *Drawing is the beginning of everything.*'[74]

This undisputed master of the aesthetics of disappearance seemed not to know that, from now on, *no beginning would be guaranteed.*[75] For some fifty years, in fact, drawing has been banished from the walls of art galleries, and now it is painting's turn to be considered the technical vestige of another era.

The museomania of the poor was not, then, to spare the privileged, and this would be another meaning of **big optics**: multinational powers aiming for a monopoly of the market in appearances; capitalists no longer rushing for gold, but for the totality of the world's images.

---

74 From the catalogue of the exhibition to mark Giacometti's centenary, Centre Pompidou, Winter 2001.

75 Paul Virilio, *The Aesthetics of Disappearance* (New York: Semiotext(e), 1994).

After Ted Turner of CNN, Bill Gates would get in on the act and declare: 'It's possible, you can never know, that the universe exists only for me. If so, it's sure going well for me, I must admit.'[76]

As consenting victims of contemporary solipsism, the Guggenheims, for their part, are expecting to reign supreme over a **global** museum. Similarly, we were to learn that, in the Berlusconi government's Finance Bill for 2002, the management of museums, archives, libraries and archaeological sites would be handed over in its entirety to the Italian private sector for a five-year rental of 160 million euros . . . .

All this gives an unexpected meaning to a recent text in which an art critic commented on *a new way of consuming art thanks to the Internet*, and, secondarily, a new way of ensuring the economic survival of authors who would not really be authors since, as in the way the rights to electronic games are tied up, they would no longer be the exclusive owners of their works.

In keeping with the criteria prevailing in the *electro-optical economy*, this new art could in future be regarded as a 'service to society' and these artists, by being admitted to the status of *researchers*, could be sponsored by multinationals for two or three years with an *obligation to publish* – exactly, we are told, as happens in the scientific world.[77]

Another prominent example of this palace revolution, the Paris School of Political Sciences, has announced that its students will in future be trained in 'the management of cultural

76 Walter Isaacson, 'In Search of the Real Bill Gates', *Time*, vol. 149, no. 2, 13 January 1997.
77 Michel Nuridsany, 'Internet, la grande rupture', *Le Figaro*, 8 September 2000.

enterprises', while the great hall of the École des hautes études commerciales at Jouy-en-Josas, traditionally reserved for the end-of-year ball, has been rechristened 'Contemporary Art Space'.

This arrangement, which will involve the staging of two exhibitions a year, will be rounded off with artists in residence – a further indication of the replacement of true art lovers and the old gallery owners by transnational managers.

As wedding presents in these unnatural marriages of a kind that have long been solemnized in the United States – Yale, Austin or Berkeley possessing important contemporary collections – our artists would no doubt be required urgently to provide for their new sponsors their power of terroristic change, their meta-design.

This privatization – or, if you prefer, takeover – of the world's appearances had begun in the nineteenth century when, on the Romantic pretext of saving cathedrals from demolition, medieval art and architecture had been disfigured, adapting them to the *machinistic* taste of the engineers. Today it is the turn of the restorers, makeover artists and scientific experts of all kinds to get their hands on the *biodiversity* of a European art in which the gods assumed a human face, in which the museums were simply the temples of a Graeco-Latin and Judeao-Christian anthropocentrism.[78]

To enter the race of economic globalism is then also, for

---

78 Compare also the attitude of the Roman Church in the 'iconoclast crisis' and at the Second Council of Nicaea (787), where *the legitimacy of images and their worship* was decided, 'the Christ of the Incarnation having built a bridge between the visible and the invisible'.

the *compradores* of the Old World, to throw off the cumbersome burden of their own culture. To be convinced of this, we need only listen once again to Christophe Girard of the Paris city authority announcing that there will be dancing in the Louvre where the Rembrandts hang, and – why not, after that? – in churches kept open at night for the purpose . . . .

Apart from obvious economic and strategic considerations, one might also see this as one of the causes of the recent moral abandonment of the state of Israel by its traditional allies and systems of information whose traditional task it is to invent every new enemy, every possible accident or crime.

But let us listen to Joseph Roth observing, on the eve of the first total war in contemporary history: 'In the eyes of the Hitlerian pagans, it is not just the Jews, but the Christians too who are the children of Israel, and it is clear to anyone who has eyes to see that anti-Semitism is a pretext and what we have here is, in reality, an anti-Christianism. During the Third Reich they started with the boycotting of Jewish shops and went on to boycott Christian churches. They spat on the star of David in order to attack the Cross.'[79]

Let us also look clear-sightedly at what is currently going on: Jewish and Christian graves profaned by 'calculated satanic acts', corpses desecrated, synagogues and churches set on fire in our suburbs . . . the new routine of a local terrorism, systematically ignored by the mass media.

And the manoeuvres of the French Prime Minister Lionel Jospin, also spring to mind, calling up as he did the President

79 Joseph Roth, *Das journalistische Werk*. Quoted here from the French translation, *Automne à Berlin* (Paris: Éditions de la Quinzaine/Louis Vuitton, 2000) p. 231.

of the European Convention, Roman Herzog, to declare the reference to the religious heritage of Europe in the Charter of Fundamental Rights '*unacceptable*' (European Agency press release, 14 September 2000).

Yet, on the eve of the Christian festival of All Saints, Halloween is celebrated in our schools, with its cortege of ghosts, witches and satanaels[80] . . . some even going so far as to propose the cancellation of the Christmas festival and its seasonal rejoicing in favour of that commercial masquerade of which 'Satan is the only God!'

So, when our cultural spokesmen, such as Jean-Pierre Mohen, announce that they have, in their field, to make *political choices*, we shall understand them to mean *transpolitical choices*.

As we saw in the laborious negotiations of the 1995 GATT round, the conversion to planetary economy required the absolute conformity of all goods *without any cultural exception*.

The **nothing but the Earth**[81] of globalism, showing itself gradually for what it is: a return to sender of the old *colonial slave code* which laid down that *no durable civilization must be allowed to constitute itself in the colonies*.

---

80 Satanael is the name given to Lucifer in Manichaean mythology. In Hans-Jürgen Heinrichs's interview with Cioran, which the author quotes above, Cioran also says: 'I have always found the idea attractive that it wasn't God, but Satan, a little Satan, Satanael, who created the world.' [Trans.]

81 This is an allusion to Paul Morand's book *Rien que la terre* (Paris: Grasset, 1926) [Trans.].

*

'Tomorrow you will all be Negroes!' prophesied James Baldwin, turning American racism round against its perpetrators.[82]

In the early years of the twentieth century, art lovers and gallery owners should have been on their guard against what the Cubists, the Expressionists and the mass media crudely dubbed '*art nègre*' or '*art négro-africain*'. This was predominantly an *airport art*, a commodity from nowhere and no one, to be consumed by anyone at all.

The *art nègre* art object – and its masks which no longer had any actual faces behind them – was a warning to the artists of a Europe which was then still colonial. It heralded their imminent identification with the artists of *voiceless peoples, who are no longer permitted to be conscious of, and take any pride in, themselves*.[83]

From the 1950s onwards, with the coming of decolonization, we were to discover the transcultural and transpolitical power of the new global markets.

Nuclear power, for example, where it was difficult to distinguish what was commercial (power stations) from what was military (the bomb), despite the risk of the technology

---

82 In *The Fire Next Time* (London: Penguin Books in association with Michael Joseph, 1964), Baldwin writes: 'The white man's unadmitted – and apparently, to him, unspeakable – private fears and longings are projected on to the Negro. The only way he can be released from the Negro's tyrannical power over him is to consent, in effect, to become black himself' (p. 82). And in his last essay, 'Whose Harlem is this anyway?' he writes: 'The profit motive makes everyone a nigger or a nigger's overseer' [Trans.].

83 Caspar David Friedrich.

spreading to terrorists, which was to be reckoned with even then.

Similarly, the future of the vital markets of energy, information and the biotechnologies was already mapped out: it would accompany the drift towards the wholesale disappearance of *raison d'État* and its replacement by a multitude of transnational networks. The politico-economic scandals of the late twentieth century have reminded us once again – democracies die, sooner or later, from the secret duplication of state services.

But what is concealed today behind the cracked façade of our republican constitutions?

The tragic events in New York in September 2001 showed us the alarming situation of an overpowerful state suddenly brought up short against its own consciousness – or, rather, against *its techno-scientific unconsciousness*: in other words, against the Gnosticist faith on which it is founded.

Let us not forget that, since the inopportune pursuit of the Manhattan Project by American physicists,[84] the scientific 'sorcerer's spirit' had found itself virtually released from the authority of its former patrons and, particularly, of their axiomatics – the ideological, social, economic and cultural criteria – on which the authority of the State was founded. And that had led to Hiroshima.

A purified dystopia, a watertight system in which, after the collapse of the old epistemological ambitions, the scientist,

---

84 'There was a moment in the history of humanity when mankind could have taken a quite other path and no atomic arsenal would ever have seen the light of day. That moment very much depended on the behaviour of a handful of scientists who were, for the most part, left-wing humanists . . . . But all of them, without exception, continued their work imperturbably' (Charles Mopsik).

stripped of his civilizational attributes, *would work only for the scientist, each discovery grafting itself on to the previous one and science finding the sources and ends of its existence on its own ground*, like the Jehova of Genesis![85]

This lends another meaning, for example, to the remarks of the Franco-Iranian philosopher Daryush Shayegan, who told a journalist: 'To speak of civilizations as blocs counterposed to one other without interpenetration is an illusion.' He went on to say: '*We are all Westerners.*' And he analysed the subtle relations between Islamism and an omnipresent Marxism in the Third World in the postcolonial period – relations he referred to as a *Bolshevization of religion*.

In fact, in general pan-Islamic terrorism one can see straight away Arab (or other) multinationals exploiting the beliefs or hatred of a global subproletariat, a lumpen class produced by decolonization and mass immigration, but one sees also an elite of rich Muslim students, military men and technicians (pilots, programmers, scientists, etc.) who, as is immediately noticeable, resemble in every particular the suicidal members of the American 'Heaven's Gate' cybersect.

To speak, as Daryush Shayegan does, of *the light which comes from the West*, and of *a world which will not be able to escape Progress*, is to fall inadvertently into the biblical company of Lucifer (the Bearer of Light), into the tragic irony of Dürer's **Melancholia**, and to forget that the Judaeo-Christian story of Genesis is *the story of a scientific suicide*.

As I have written elsewhere, in emancipating itself from politics, faith in progress has entered the field of pure strategy –

85 Here I have adapted a phrase of Schlegel's.

the essence of war – the pure strategy of the nuclear status quo.

Like the illusionism to which it owes a great debt, techno-scientific development has become an **art of the false** in the service of the **art of the lie** – a series of manipulations of appearances, tricks and, in some cases, a tissue of absurdities.[86]

When, during the Cold War, the talk was of the **society of the spectacle**, of politics-as-spectacle or alienation to commercialism, what was mainly at issue was the spectacular revolution of an informational complex moving, over a few decades, from the old totalitarian threats to global threats, from Leninist electrification to the global electronic field.

So, when Bill Joy, at the end of the last century, carried out his informal survey among specialists in the most powerful technologies, he introduced us to a curious melting-pot, running from the inevitable superman to Isaac Asimov's robot cycle, Michelangelo or the paths of Buddhism . . . but, first and foremost, to fiction, mainly through productions made for TV, the aesthetic aberrations of the current techno-science futurologists presenting frequent similarities with **Star Trek** or *Alien*.[87]

We had moved, then, from the realism and the rationalist logic of the printed word, and the Jules Verne-type *novel of scientific prediction*, to the teratological phantasmagorias of science-fiction scenarios aimed at the industrial cinema, before these latter were in their turn eliminated by the telescoping, in the new popular cinema, of special effects, whose instantaneity

86 Sun Tzu: 'Strategy is the art of lying.'
87 Joy, 'Why the future doesn't need us'. In that article, Bill Joy informs us of his immediate hopes of participating in a wider discussion with individuals from various different horizons in a cast of mind free both from the fear and from the idolizing of technology.

and interactivity exclude any coherent narrative whatsoever, with the spectator no longer being provided with any kind of verisimilitude, but fed exclusively on the *exhibition of accidents*.

It will also be noticed that once this stage of the *meaninglessness of the visible world* was reached, the (American, Asian and other) *dream factories* rapidly laid off a large number of original authors and screenwriters who were regarded as unproductive. Shortly afterwards, we were to see the failure of 'Sillywood'. After being announced in 1992 as the 'new golden age of entertainment', the marriage between Silicon Valley and Hollywood was to end in failure after a few short months – partly for want of a common strategy, but mainly for want of *content*.

'When nothingness becomes reality, reality in its turn tips over into nothingness,' stated the old strategist.

It will be hard to grasp anything of the various expansionist comments currently being heard around the world if we do not keep firmly in mind the oft-neglected fact that every technology expresses itself in its time as a *new field of force*.

Here as elsewhere, what is troubling about the covert state of transnational terrorism – that unknown quantity – is its growing subordination to a techno-scientific progress which is, itself, unauthored and dependent on the development of its own audiovisual media and platforms.

The scientific imagination ultimately suffers the same fate as 'e-tainment'; it comes to resemble that of those TV viewers who thought the attack on the World Trade Center on September 11 was merely another disaster movie, or that of the Islamist suicide-attackers no doubt dying happy at becoming actors in a global super-production in which *reality would tip over* once and for all *into electronic nothingness*.

6

The intermittent, violent terror of
exceptional epidemics had given way to
the constant fear of ordinary endemics
which had until then passed unnoticed.

LÉON BERNARD

The totalitarianisms of the twentieth century could not have
been established if, as his minister Albert Speer noted of him,
Hitler had not been a peerless psychologist who had known
how to exploit the most modern technologies to the full.

Others claim that Hitler was the greatest ad man of his age,
since his logo alone – the swastika – is still as effective as ever.

However, in one of his short stories, Isaac Asimov points
out that, long before the arrival of the Nazis, the swastika
was regarded in Germany as a lucky charm, like the four-
leaved clover or the rabbit's foot. It might be said, then, to
have been the skilful exploitation of superstitious fears that
ultimately gave a sacred character to the grandiose liturgies of
Nuremberg . . . .

Hannah Arendt, for her part, commenting on a passage in *Mein Kampf* (Book 1, Chapter 11), noted: 'The strong emphasis of totalitarian propaganda on the "scientific" nature of its assertions has been compared to certain advertising techniques which also address themselves to masses.'[88] And Arendt stressed the fact that if Nazi propaganda had learnt a lot from American commercial advertising, the latter borrowed most of its methods from gangsterism, and those kinds of Mafia-style offers which no one can safely refuse.

Hence the apparently trivial example of an advertisement for soap chosen by Hitler to illustrate his argument, the kind of advertising which exploits the fear of contamination and epidemic, and which, though claiming to be based on 'the latest scientific discoveries', is merely a vehicle for the fear of grave social and health consequences (premature ageing, skin diseases, not to mention an unhappy love life and losing one's job).

Thus the example given by Hitler as a model of totalitarian propaganda – that of an apparently frivolous advertisement – was perfectly suited to what was, in his view, a goal of vital importance.[89]

Still to talk about *civilization*, when sites of a new *cultural management* aimed at combining art with Science and advertising are repeatedly being uncovered, is to participate in its liquidation.

88 Arendt, *The Origins of Totalitarianism*, p. 345.
89 'Scientificality of mass propaganda has indeed been so universally employed in modern politics that it has been interpreted as a more general sign of that obsession with science which has characterized the Western world since the rise of mathematics and physics in the sixteenth century; thus totalitarianism appears to be only the last stage in a process during which "science [has become] an idol that will magically cure the evils of existence and transform the nature of man".' (Arendt, *The Origins of Totalitarianism*, p. 346).

We are told, in fact, that we now have to look for artistic creation elsewhere than in the old monodisciplinary spectacles. Today the theatre or dance companies find themselves forced, in their turn, to enter the category of exports/services, and to conform to the norms of the global endocolony or disappear with the technical remnants of another age . . . after painters, sculptors and architects . . . .

Meanwhile, heartened by the 'new deal' of an *authorless culture*, university teachers, bio-informaticians and biochemists collaborate actively in these new spectacles, designing scenarios which, in their view, *enable them to embrace a wider audience* – for example, the scenarios of 'genetic serials', aimed primarily at secondary-school students, in which the visual arts and contemporary music and dance make up, alongside the techno-sciences, a 'mosaic landscape'.

After compulsory sex education in schools, we are now seeing the promotion of an artistic scientism and its specialities (genetics, nanotechnology and robotics), all with a fine economic future before them, not forgetting also the global success of new computerized toys like tamagochi, which give children the sense of controlling the life and death of an electronic infant at will.

But let us review once again the course of this other history of Art. We shall see there the promised end of major international events like IMAGINA, which have become resounding economic failures. For thirty years they had had the task of promoting the ultimate twinning of art and high technology. In fact, video art and its countless installations implicitly cast into doubt our sensible presence here and now, in favour of a hypothetical instantaneous presence everywhere and nowhere. An art of dislocation and multi-location somewhat reminiscent of the anxieties of those characters in search of an author of the Pirandellian theatre of the 1930s.

After the economic collapse of that discreet deportation, the next phase was that of the great game of disappearance, which would consist in getting rid of bodies, which had become an encumbrance. As though, with the **body world** of global endocolonialism succeeding the **body politic** of the old democracies, this future body world required the creation of a **body art** and a biological body which, in short order, should come to resemble, like a clone, the body of Baldwin's Negro or, even better, take its inspiration from the 'Revolutionary catechism' of the old Russian anarchists, and be the body of someone who 'would have no personal interest, no business, no feelings, no ties, no property, not even a name that was his own . . .'.

The avant-garde of current art was not, then, Nam June Paik and his many imitators, but the Viennese Actionists of the 1960s and their bloody rituals in which animals were tortured to death, and the Judaeo-Christian symbols of an execrated anthropocentrism were profaned. Cultural subproducts reviving the masochistic rites of the congregations of crucified and flagellants, or the suicidal rites of the fanatical followers of Jagannath. The main value of the photogenic exactions of the Danubian celebrants was to effect a conversion to an academicism of crime and abjection which, ceasing to be marginal, was to invade an increasing number of official art events and *biennales*.

Here again we see the evolutionary continuity of a culture of a Sadeian type imposing itself, a culture which might be said itself to be merely a neurotic double of the religion of progress.

The Pop Art of the New Deal of the 1930s and that of the 1950s, the American hyperrealism or counterculture of the industrial consumer society (painted plaster hamburgers, tins of sausages) would give way to the plastinated bodies of an ultimate *exploitation of man by man* – that of industrial biotechnology. With no origins, no fixed abode and no identity, beyond the common mortuary and the mass grave – the programmed culmination of the art of portraiture, if not, indeed, of the Identikit portrait . . . .

But the exhibiting of these anatomical specimens will put us most in mind of the mass health promotions with which we have become familiar, thanks to the international success of paramedical television programmes of the kind many countries broadcast on World AIDS Day. Here again, the development of the pedagogical-promotional will is clear: from the exemplary case of sexually transmitted diseases, in which bodies previously admired and desired, then indifferently exchanged and prostituted, will come in the end to be regarded as epidemiological risk factors, defying any sexual appetite and, before long, any pity, we move on through the public's disaffection with AIDS fashion and its logos, to the promotion of the 'genetics as catch-all explanation' message, bringing into the TV studios unfortunates suffering from rare – and previously incurable – hereditary diseases . . . new, barely concealed eugenic threats.

And it will not be long before a transgenic art makes its appearance, in order, we are told, 'to acquaint people with artificial life, that discipline which combines the scientific, technological and artistic fields with the aim of studying life by computer simulations, robotic constructions or genetic manipulations . . . . If artificial life explores life as it is, it also explores forms of life as they could be.'[90]

90 These words are taken from the presentation of an event named *Vie*

And Professor Günther von Hagen will again be in the news, the inventor of a so-called *aesthetic* plastination of human corpses, who recently saw fit to add to the set of bodies he exhibits that of a four-month-old foetus in the open belly of its mother, and a 'cabinet of horrors' in which the public may discover a batch of misshapen human embryos.[91]

The point, in all these cases, is to inspire repulsion and contempt for *sui generis* organisms in the general public, which is initially attracted by their obscenity, and to do so by showing those organisms subjected to degrading treatment – particularly the bodies of young children or newborn infants. A call to a new massacre of the innocents, innocent but *presumed guilty* of reminding us of the laws of natural procreation – the laws, too, of a Love which, as Marcel Proust has it, makes *space and time perceptible to the heart*.[92]

But we shall see, above all, the fearful splitting of a constitutional state divided against itself.[93]

Article 4 of the European Union's Charter of Fundamental Rights stipulates that 'No one shall be subjected to torture or to inhuman or degrading treatment or punishment.'

artificielle in Avignon on 20 October 2000. The full text is available on the website 'cafe9avignon.org' [Trans.].

91   The exploits of Günther von Hagen began in 1998 with the Körperwelten [Body Worlds] exhibition at Mannheim. Since then, his collection of corpses has increased by several thousand. See Paul Virilio, *The Information Bomb* (London and New York: Verso, 2000), p. 51.

92   This is a reference to Proust's famous line: 'L'amour, c'est l'espace et le temps rendus sensibles au coeur' (*La Prisonnière*, Paris: Gallimard, 1954, p. 464) [Trans.].

93   The French term here is 'état de droit', which implies a state obeying the rule of law roughly along the lines of the English 'constitutional state' or the German *Rechtsstaat* [Trans.].

Yet, in the year which saw the passing of the Sex Offenders Act in Great Britain, an Act intended to curb paedophilia and the sadistic industrialization of the sex trade, the first **Sensation** exhibition was held at the London Royal Academy, where pride of place among a hundred and ten works exhibited by the advertising executive Charles Saatchi went to the portrait of the child murderer Myra Hindley throned in majesty.

Offshore zones, zones beyond the reach of law? The official biennales and the art galleries now set themselves up as partners to transnational organizations, braving all laws, all taboos. While advertising men, like the famous Ottaviani, whose work was once thought too shocking, now complain of being left behind.

By way of response, a famous couturier recently declared: 'I don't advertise, I create events!'

It will henceforth be the mission of *haute couture* – financed by the 'luxury sector' of the global economy – to de-ghettoize the national museums or art galleries by providing the mass media with the ultimate popular images of modernity.[94] Or, rather, *basse couture,* with its Anglo-Saxon 'bad boys' subjecting the bodies of the supermodels to a degrading sham: grunge fashion, the art-for-art's-sake of body-piercing, tattoos and scarifications.

Tomorrow you will all be Negroes. The naked bodies and flowers of Woodstock, and of the great families of rock will be replaced by the techno ritual of raves – nomadic lawless areas

---

94 Here Christophe Girard's arrival as cultural delegate of the Paris city authority assumes its full transpolitical meaning.

in which replicants delight in appearing in what lenient
authorities refer to delicately as *undignified postures*!

'Admittedly, there was 'body art' which, acting in a violent
way on bodies, sought to overturn the old principles by hang-
ing from butchers' hooks. . . . But this is as nothing compared
with the impact of current artists who take their interventions
on bodies to paroxystic heights.' This comparative advertising
of a new type is taken from an article devoted to the presentation of Spring–Summer fashions for 2001 which appeared in
the *Journal du dimanche*.

The move from a Stelarc some ten years ago telling *L'Autre
Journal*: 'I try to extend the capacities of the body using technology. For example, I use medical techniques, sound
systems, a robotic hand, an artificial arm. . . . It is, in fact, the
interweaving of these voluntary, involuntary and programmed
movements which seems interesting to me', to *self-hybridations*
of the kind practised by Orlan, yielding her inert body to
Baroque surgical mutilations carried out by peculiar aesthetic
surgeons, renders the word 'performance' no longer applica-
ble in this rush of plasticians towards the laboratories of a
biocracy that is now routinely accepted.

7

What is a crime in a country where
there is no longer any law?

LIEUTENANT-COLONEL ROBIN HODGES,
(British Officer in charge of the
Central Sector of Kosovo)

From the nation to the world city, from geopolitics to metro-
politics? As in the American megalopolises, the frontiers now
run inside European cities. Each area, each district, is becoming a forbidden territory occupied by an ethnic group foreign
to the others, clashing over a building or a street corner.

Resettlement territories, comparable to those of the old
colonies, with their social dissidents expelled from Europe –
religious or political exiles, sectarians, proletarians, convicts,
delinquents, prostitutes . . . urban zones where *the margin
becomes the mass*.

But let us listen to Jean de Maillard denouncing the way-
ward drift into a 'lawless world': 'The first phenomena of
destabilization date in France from the 1970s, with instances

of fraud in the world of work, false subcontracting, endless social deregulation . . .'. And he adds: '*I could already feel the deregulation of the world coming*.'[95]

For Judge Maillard, Bin Laden's planes are merely boomerangs – 'tell me your crimes and I'll tell you who you are' – and the terrorist phenomenon begins in everyday life.

In fact, this commonplace destabilization had its origins in Europe as early as the First World War, particularly with the maritime blockade inflicted on Germany by the Allies – a blockade which was to leave the country economically and morally drained, thus allowing the irresistible rise of a totalitarian power of the gangster type, as described by Brecht.

Twenty years later, on the occasion of a total war where 'every moral consideration was officially set aside' by each of the adversaries, we would see a proliferation of illegal trafficking, black-marketeering and crimes of all kinds, of 'everything which allows the dignity of man to disappear irredeemably', as Georges Bernanos observed.

But, above all, let us not forget that in the twentieth century, the emulation of the battlefield seemed essential to the fanatical advocates of techno-scientific Progress, who saw that progress as *an assault on nature*.

For example, Père Teilhard de Chardin – that strange Jesuit who claimed to have discovered, in the great massacres of the First World War, 'the face of the unfinished man of evolution' – noted in 1955: '*War is an organic phenomenon of anthropogenesis* which Christianity can no more eliminate than death.'

This explains a posteriori the arrogant attitude of the

95 Jean de Maillard, *Un monde sans loi* (Paris: Stock, 1998).

defendants in the Nuremberg trials, who took the view that they had merely been obeying the laws of a scientific bio-ethic, and did not in any way feel responsible for the crimes they had committed: were not European peoples then *in a time of war*, and hence automatically deprived of most of their civil rights? Had not the German state, by virtue of the acknowledged rules, the power to drive them hither and thither at will, from massacre on the battlefields to slaughter in the strategic bombing of the great cities or the labour camps?

And the revolutionary decimations of the twentieth century – the century of barbed wire and camps[96] – can also be seen in terms of an extension of *experimental* (economic, scientific and biological) *zones* outside the law– from that month of August 1918 when Lenin called for 'dubious elements' to be quarantined, and Trotsky created the first concentration camps for 'parasites' on the outskirts of towns.

Today, must we fear the creation of artificial conditions of civil war in Europe within our enfeebled, senile democracies?

What are we to think of these new *resettlement operations* overseen by the multinational mafias and conducted under the auspices of the UN? These waves of panic immigration which are currently unfurling with, within their ranks, the arrival of 'people for whom war is a country and civil war a homeland' (Konrad Heiden)?

Not far from our towns and cities, camps are being built for displaced persons – in Ireland and France; at Sangatte, for example . . . .

96 Joel Kotek and Pierre Rogoulot, *Le Siècle des camps* (Paris: Jean-Claude Lattès, 2000).

Are we already seeing the first burgeonings of a global sub-humanity, of that abolition of *human beings as such* that is dreamed of by the biotechnology gurus and taken up as a task by the hoodlums of organized crime?

Will the war of each against all play a major role in a new sanitary ideology cast in the form of humanitarianism? Once again, we have to remember here the role played, since the early twentieth century, by the battlefield. With the arrival in Europe of the many philanthropic enterprises set up by the multinationals: Standard Oil, for example; or, in 1917, the Rockefeller Mission on the French front, claiming that it would eradicate tuberculosis from the country. Not forgetting those Americans who dreamed of 'universal sanitation': of the installation of a universal health police in a world linked by great bacteriological chains.[97]

Let us further remember that a Ministry of Health was created in France in the 1930s. While the Nazi government, after setting up free medical insurance enabling files to be opened on its entire population, would soon allot the task of X-raying the nation, and sending its sick to their deaths, to a medical science which had turned into a forensic medicine – here again practising an eradication worthy of veterinary prophylaxis.

Thus, *on the first day of total war,* Hitler, now confident of his rights, could at last sign the death sentence of millions of human beings who were decreed irredeemable. After the

97 See Paul Virilio, 'L'idéologie sanitaire', in *L'Insécurité du territoire.* 2nd edn (Paris: Galilée, 1993), pp. 185–93. See also Lion Murard and Patrick Zylberman, 'Les Rockefeller Medicine Men en France, 1917–1923', in Jean-Louis Cohen and Hubert Damish (eds), *Américanisme et modernité* (Paris: Presses de l'École des hautes études en sciences sociales/Flammarion, 1993).

pathogenic races (Jews, Gypsies, Slavs, etc.), it would quickly
be the turn of the mentally ill, of sexual deviants, of the disabled, then the tubercular, those suffering from heart disease,
the aged, whom the regime planned to marginalize before
proceeding to slaughter them.[98]

Should we be surprised, then, that today former concentration camp prisoners, such as Joseph Rowan, are almost the
only ones to rebel against the immense death pyres on which,
since the year 2000, hundreds of thousands of animals have
been consumed, condemned by a health measure which has
passed from prevention (BSE) to economic logic (the entirely
curable foot-and-mouth disease), with a mysterious bacteriological terrorism, then as yet in the pipeline, establishing the
veterinary relationship between animals and humans, in the
form of anthrax.

In 1993, I wrote of the first attack on the World Trade
Center: 'No matter who is responsible, it ushers in a new era
of terrorism, having nothing in common with the explosions
that regularly rock Ireland or England. Indeed, the outstand-
ing feature of the attack is that it was seriously intended to
bring down the World Trade Center building. . . . So it is . . .
*a strategic event confirming for us all the change in the military
order of this fin-de-siècle.'*[99]

---

98 Hitler had planned to introduce a 'National Health Bill' which
    would have meant that 'the number of people no longer allowed "to
    remain among the public" would have formed a considerable por-
    tion of the German population' (Arendt, *The Origins of
    Totalitarianism*, p. 416 n.)

99 Paul Virilio, *A Landscape of Events*, trans. Julie Rose (Cambridge,
    MA/London: MIT Press, 2000), p. 18. The original French article
    was published in the magazine *Globe*, 30 March 1993.

Let us make no mistake about it: with the 11 September 2001 attack, we have before us *an act of total war*, remarkably conceived and executed, with a minimum of resources. And this demonstrates something we had forgotten: that 'everything in war is very simple, but the simplest thing is difficult'.[100]

The destruction wrought on the Pentagon was of little consequence; what exploded in people's minds was the World Trade Center, leaving America out for the count.

The business of America being business – and, principally, world business – it is in fact *the apparent economy of the planet* which finds itself lastingly affected here by the dystopia of its own system.

On September 11 2001, the Manhattan skyline became the front of the new war.

The anonymity of those who initiated the attack merely signals, for everyone, the rise of a **global covert state** – of the *unknown quantity* of a private criminality – that 'beyond-Good-and-Evil' which has for centuries been the dream of the high priests of an iconoclastic progress.

October 20 2001

100 Karl von Clausewitz, *On War*, ed. and trans Michael Howard and
Peter Paret (London: David Campbell Publishers, 1993), p. 138.